# TEST OF T...

David had been w... ever since he had g... and "expert" opinic... had sacrificed a lot ... and all the things being you... supposed to be about. Slowly his name became known through minor roles in TV. And now was his big chance – a top role on a new sure-fire hit show, *The Partridge Family*.

Then he discovered who would be starring beside him ı his stepmother, the woman who had married his father after the divorce that had shattered David's young life.

And now trying out for the role was not only a test of his talents – it was an ultimate testing of his own deepest and most painful emotions as well . . .

# The David Cassidy Story

## BY JAMES GREGORY

WORLD DISTRIBUTORS (MANCHESTER) LTD.

Published in MCMLXXIII by
World Distributors (Manchester) Ltd
12 Lever Street Manchester M60 1TS

Made and printed in Great Britain by
C. Nicholls & Company Ltd
The Philips Park Press, Manchester

SBN 7235 5000 X

*Dedication:*

This book is for Marge Gregory, Mary Kay Sprague and Leora Carpenter, the members of my family ... and also for James Davidson, who helped so much.

Some of the material in this book originally appeared in a different form in the pages of Modern Screen, Motion Picture, Photoplay, Silver Screen, TV Radio Mirror and TV Radio Talk, and the permission of these magazines to use it here is gratefully acknowledged. And for their invaluable contributions to this book, thanks also to Alex MacDonald, Duncan Lent, Judy Strangis, Dave Madden and Susan Dey . . . and above all to David Cassidy.

# CONTENTS

# JUST AMONG THE THREE OF US

I hope this book is not exactly what you expected. For if it were, it would contain no surprises. But it does.

If you expected a book that simply says, on each and every page, "David Cassidy is the greatest," then you expected a pep talk – and you don't need that. For to each of you who reads this book, David Cassidy *is* the greatest.

This book is not a biography, although most of it is in fairly chronological order.

This is just a book *about* David Cassidy – a book of many moods and revelations, ranging from hilarious to tragic. It is written from friendship, from memory . . . but mostly from David's very own words, as told to me over a period of several years, beginning when he was only 13 years old.

This book is also a conversation, just among the three of us – you and David and me. As we three sit around and rap, you'll learn countless things about David that you didn't know, as the conversation ranges freely from subject to subject, from today back to the past, then again to the present, and with several revealing looks at David's future as he and his friends see it now.

We may touch on a topic, an opinion or a memory, change the subject, and then perhaps go back later to add something you ought to know to what had been said before.

11

This book is very personal. It tries always to tell the truth, for you deserve that. And I think that as a result it is very revealing of what David Cassidy is really like.

A number of David's other friends have talked to me about him, and their information has been helpful in putting this book together. Some of their names you won't know – Alex MacDonald, Duncan Lent, Dave Madden and Susan Dey of *The Partridge Family* are also among those I interviewed, and you know them both.

Judy Strangis' name, too, is familiar to all of David's fans, for she has dated him at times and been photographed with him often. Also, she has many fans of her own because of her role on *Room 222*. When I saw how much of what Judy had told me was in this book, I was surprised for a moment. And then I realized how many fascinating and revealing facts she had provided, and I knew that the book would lose a lot if I left any of them out. For she was "there" when I was not, at an amazingly large number of important events in David's life. And what a memory that girl has!

Indeed, all of us who have known David Cassidy from his earliest adolescence to the years of his young manhood and stardom find it hard to forget anything about him. For he has always been a most unusual, highly interesting and altogether memorable person – even though, at the same time, he was also just "one of the gang" and didn't seem slated for stardom.

All of us who know him, and whose experiences and conversations with him are in this book, have tried to "tell it like David is." And I am sure he would only want it to be that way.

So if by chance you plan to be a star, and expect to have a book written about you someday, do what David Cassidy did years ago, when he was in his early teens. Pick a lot of friends with good memories. If one of them happens to be a professional writer, so much the better.

And then just be yourself around them ... and tell them

from the very beginning of your friendship just what you're thinking, and how you feel about life. But if you think they might kid you about wanting to be a star, play that down.

Yes, come to think of it, all that is *exactly* what David did. Do you think he knew something that the rest of us didn't?

## Chapter One

# THE TEENAGE DAVID CASSIDY I KNEW

"What do you want to be?" I asked 15-year-old David Cassidy one day back in 1965. I'll never forget his answer – because it surprised me so.

"I want to be an actor," he told me hesitantly.

I had known David for over two years, and he had never said anything before about going into show business. And what's more, he didn't seem to me to have the necessary gifts for success – even though he came from a show-business family.

He was average-looking, really – except for those huge, thickly-lashed hazel eyes of his, eyes that looked like something out of a Keane painting. They resembled the eyes of his father, Jack Cassidy, the Broadway and television star. But there the resemblance ended.

Jack was a talented, self-confident actor and singer. But as for David – well, I had never seen him perform, and he seemed so shy and soft-spoken that I couldn't imagine him ever getting up in public and trying to do so.

"He'll never make it!" I thought to myself.

But Dave was a friend, and I didn't want to hurt his feelings. So I didn't say anything against this wild idea of his, though I felt that nothing would ever come of it.

Yet even then, David was unpredictable in ways. Although he was quiet and well-behaved most of the time, he had a mischievous streak and was fond of practical jokes, as were the boys he hung around with at the time in Westwood, a Los Angeles suburb. But there was still that occasional air of sadness and isolation about him that tended to make you forgive any misbehavior – until the next time.

I was living in Westwood and David lived in nearby

Cheviot Hills when I first met him, early in 1963. A friend of his named Alex MacDonald, whose family I knew, was clipping newspaper and magazine articles for my files. One day Alex brought David along to keep him company.

After that, David took to dropping by occasionally to visit, raid the icebox, and avail himself of the chance to talk over his problems with an adult who was not a parent – something that seems important to many teenagers. This happened on and off for the next two or three years.

One day, when he was 15, David asked me: "Jim, would you teach me how to drive?"

Reluctantly – with visions of a wrecked car and canceled insurance – I agreed to teach him in my 1964 Chevelle. I drove him to an empty parking lot in Century City one evening, let him take over the wheel, and sat in the passenger's seat and watched nervously as he slowly drove around and around the lot with nary a slip. My car survived the lesson in good shape, and so did I.

Jack Cassidy had been divorced by David's mother, talented musical-comedy star Evelyn Ward, when David was only six years old, following a long separation during which Jack had fallen in love with blonde, beautiful Shirley Jones. Shirley had recently achieved stardom in the film version of the musical hit, *Oklahoma!* when they met while co-starring in a travelling company of the same show.

Jack married Shirley when his divorce became final, and they had two sons at the time I first knew David. (They now have a third.) They lived not far away from David, who lived with his mother and his stepfather, director Elliot Silverstein, whom Evelyn had married when David was 11. Silverstein directed *Cat Ballou.*

"I go to visit my dad and Shirley on weekends, and they're always very nice to me," David once told me. "But I always feel like a visitor, not a member of the family. It's not their fault. It's just how I feel. After all, I don't live with them. . . ."

Adding to his frustration – although he never mentioned
16

this to me at the time – was the fact that he wanted to be an actor and singer, like his father. But he was not permitted to try his luck in show business by his parents. They insisted that he finish high school first. Then, if he wanted to, he could seek a career in show business – but not before.

David's parents were trying to shield him from the pitfalls of the entertainment business, which they knew all too well from personal experience. And they wanted him to obtain at least the basics of a good education before he tried for a career. But their insistence that he wait was still difficult for him to accept.

Although he had sung in a church choir and had been allowed to play small parts with his mother in summer stock when he was nine, plus some TV "soap opera" work when he was ten, this only served to whet his desire to become a performer like his parents.

But he never spoke to me of his summer stock or TV experience when I first knew him, during those years in Westwood. That was why, when he told me of his dreams of being a performer, I frankly doubted that he would ever make it.

Fadeout. Fade in five years later – the summer of 1970. I walked into a banquet room at the Continental Hyatt House on Sunset Boulevard, where a party was being held to honor the stars of ABC-TV's new series, *The Partridge Family*, which was scheduled to go on the air that fall. The stars: Shirley Jones and – David Cassidy.

I wish I could have told the world, "I told you so." But at least I had never told David, "Forget it!"

We renewed acquaintances at the party, for I hadn't seen him since moving away from Westwood four years earlier. I was delighted to see that David had grown into a poised young man.

But we had an awful lot of catching up to do, so we met a few weeks later for a longer talk on the set of *The Partridge Family*, which was being filmed by Screen Gems.

I had been asked to do an interview with David for a

17

magazine article. And let me tell you that it's strange, very strange, going in to interview a neighborhood kid who has become a star.

Indeed, he had already become a teenage idol as well, with his picture on a flock of teen magazine covers and a number of records to his credit. There was even a press agent present to sit in on the conversation.

But if the situation was strange, David was no stranger. We picked up the threads of the past as if they had never been dropped, except that now we were two adults talking, for he was 20 years old. Despite the passage of time, old friends and events long past were brought into the conversation as easily as though nothing had changed.

Yet everything had changed, including David – and it was all for the better. In five years he had gone from obscurity to stardom, and in his family life the roles had been ironically reversed.

For now he and Shirley Jones were together daily on the set, and he was playing her son – while her real sons were at home, feeling a bit left out because, despite their pleas, their mother wouldn't permit them to appear on the show with her.

Yesterday's outsider was very much "in" now – and loving it!

"How did this all come about?" I asked David. I had read various accounts of how he had been cast in *The Partridge Family*, but I wanted to hear the full story from David himself – whom everybody now seemed to be calling David, until I began doing it sometimes too.

I told him about a conversation that I'd had with Shirley Jones at the *Partridge Family* party. "Shirley told me that they took each of you aside separately after Shirley Jones had agreed for David Cassidy to be up for the role, and asked if you'd mind working with one another. In fact, she told me that they asked you, 'Do you hate your stepmother?' Just what happened?"

"My manager, Ruth Aarons sent me up for the part,"

David said, "and I went to two interviews and a final reading – and they got down to two people."

He explained, "You know, they really *are* skeptical about personal relationships like Shirley's and mine in business, because it's difficult to work with two people who do not get along personally. And I can *see* why they were careful about it. It's fortunate that we do get along so well and have such a good rapport."

"Of course, you must see more of her now than you did," I noted.

He grinned happily. "Sure – every day! It's really incredible. We've got a great friendship going, and that's really nice."

"When Shirley first became your stepmother, though, did you feel somewhat resentful of her at first, thinking perhaps, 'Daddy would still be married to my mother if it weren't for her?'"

"Sure!" he admitted instantly. "I'm sure *every* kid does. But you know, I was expecting to see the wicked stepmother. And when you take a look at her, she's a –"

"Fairy godmother?"

"Yeah – super! She really is," he said enthusiastically. "And I could find nothing to make up about her in my mind, either. I couldn't even make up the fact that she was horrible, because she was so pleasant and so sweet. It was like, 'Be mean to me, I want to sulk!'"

"Did you ever let her see that?"

"No. Actually it wasn't even really there the first time. I liked her immediately. There was no uneasiness about it. She always liked me – she *seemed* to – and I always liked her.

"So we've always had a great rapport, for what it could have been. Like, when I was younger, of course, I was seven years old when I met her. So how good a rapport could she have with me?

"But as I got older, we became closer," he added. "And now she's really one of my closest friends."

19

Suddenly another thought occurred to me. "Did you worry about any backlash when your real mother saw how well you were getting along with Shirley?" I wondered.

"No, because she accepted it. She really did. It was very comfortable as far as that was concerned," David assured me

"Getting back to what you told me in Westwood about your visits to your father and Shirley in those days, I remember you told me that they were always nice to you, but you felt, here was a family – a unit – and you would come in on weekends. And, as much as they accepted you and were nice to you, you felt a bit like an outsider."

"Right! You know, I had never lived with them. So even though I was close, I never really was part of the family," he agreed. "I wasn't there every day *participating*."

And now I learned for the first time that the years immediately after I lost touch with Dave had been the most difficult of his life. He came to feel increasingly frustrated with school. And the failure of his mother's marriage to Elliot Silverstein at just that time made his misery complete. For he had liked Elliot.

David wanted very much to be in show business, yet he was forced to stay in high school by the law, which said he had to attend school until he was 18, and by his parents' insistence that he finish high school becore trying for a career.

And he found his classes very dull. He was attending a very large school – University High in West Los Angeles – and he felt like just another number there.

Unhappy at school, his family life torn up again, David began to cut classes. "I had no interest in school – I became lost!" he told me. His problems added to his mother's heartbreak, but neither of them could seem to help the other.

Hanging around with the gang, getting nothing done – that became a way of life for David. He knew it wasn't getting him anywhere, that it was hurting him – yet anything

20

seemed better than those high-school classes, which he found dull and tedious and far removed from his real interests.

Things got so bad that he was transferred to another Los Angeles high school, Hamilton High. He was in a "continuation school" class which met from 1:15 p.m. to 4 p.m. every day and was filled with students like himself – people who had no real interest in school. Yet had to attend it because they were under 18. Now he was attending classes, at least. But his heart wasn't in it, and he accomplished nothing. What the school was teaching, at least in David's particular class, seemed to him to have nothing to do with his real interests – acting and singing. He was a boy struggling to achieve an identity, to learn who he was and to become himself. But he was unable to do it.

Yet he never gave up his dreams of success in show business, even though he was doing nothing at the time to make those dreams a reality. Some inner faith in himself kept him from giving up completely, even though he had fallen into a deep gloom and a paralyzing inertia. And he continued to hang out with the wrong people – the same ones he had known at University High.

But a three-month siege of mononucleosis when he was in the eleventh grade suddenly cut off all contact with his friends and gave him a chance to think about the mess he was making of his life. As he lay in bed day after day, he saw clearly what kind of human being he was becoming, and he didn't like what he saw. He determined to change completely – and somehow, with what moral and physical strength he had left, he managed to do it.

When he recovered from his illness, he didn't take up again with his old crowd. He spent the summer between his junior and senior years doing what he had wanted to for so long – acting and singing with the Los Angeles Theatre Company, with whom he did a play and a musical.

At last he was able to do what he loved, and it was a restorative. For the first time, he was becoming himself.

21

He capped his high school career by transferring to Rexford, a superior private school in Beverly Hills, for his senior year. There he studied – *really* studied – and he graduated in 1968.

Two weeks after graduation, David moved to New York to embark on his show business career, and there he began to mend some family fences.

"Shirley and my father had a castle up in Irvington-on-the-Hudson – a real castle! And I stayed with them there," he told me. "I had a guest house in the back. So it was really nice, you know? They couldn't hear me if I screamed at the top of my lungs. I was working with a vocal coach in New York; his name was Jim Gregory, just like yours. I was working out material for auditions and things, so I would practice in the guest house.

"For the first time, I was living with my father and Shirley, and it was a nice experience," he said happily. "It was too bad it didn't happen a little earlier, though, because at that point I didn't *want* to be with anybody, really.

"I was really away from them still, because I worked all day at a job in the garment district in New York City, and studied singing after work, and I came back at night."

Yet he *was* living with his father and stepmother, and it was a rewarding experience. "I was a little skeptical of my father at first," he confessed. "But Shirley had *always* been my friend.

"It was a little different with my father. I didn't really know how to adjust to him, but it was the best thing for me. It really helped me to grow up out of that adolescent thing. And I took on a lot of self-respect, a lot of responsibility. I was able to deal with a lot of my problems better. Yes, I think it was a good experience for me."

Making the experience even more rewarding was Shirley Jones, who quietly went about building bridges of communication between her husband, who tended to be a strict father, and her stepson, who was anxious to spread his wings and achieve maturity and independence. She was

22

several years younger than Jack Cassidy and only a few years older than David, so she had ways of helping to bridge the generation gap that an older woman might not have possessed. Added to this advantage were her own naturaly qualities of compassion and understanding, which were put to good use in the situation in which she found herself.

"Did you take your dad's advice when he offered it?" I asked David.

"A certain amount of it. A certain amount I threw away because it wasn't right for me," he admitted. "I suppose that's *always* the case, you know?"

"What is his reaction to you at this point, now that your career has taken off?" I wondered.

"Well, we've never really discussed our careers," David said. "*His* career, I know, has had its high points and its low points, and I'd say that now he's really coming into his own. He's doing a lot of films now. He's always been there. It's just a matter of the public sort of finding out what he had.

"I know that there's a lot of frustration involved," David continued, with surprising frankness. "I think he finds it a little hard to cope with the fact that Shirley found it easy to break into what she did. It was never really rough for her.

"And it was never really rough for me, either," he added. "Shirley and I both happen to be individuals who are fortunate – Shirley even more so than me, probably, because she broke into a feature film from nothing, you know. And it was like the biggest motion picture on the whole lot – *Oklahoma!* It was amazing.

"So I guess my father can find it kind of hard, because he's been in the business for 30 years, something like that, and he started as a chorus singer and has worked his way up through 30 Broadway shows, which is unbelievable!"

It only took *one* Broadway show to start things rolling for David. He was sent by his manager, Ruth Aarons, to auditions and then he landed it and only a few months after hitting New York.

David appeared with Barry Nelson and Dorothy Loudon

in a musical comedy called *The Fig Leaves Are Falling*. Although it was a fast flop, he was seen by a man from Cinema Center Films who brought him to Hollywood to test for *Hail Hero*.

David did not win a part in the picture. But while he was in Hollywood, Ruth Aarons introduced him to some people at Universal and he was cast in that studio's television show, Ironside.

His work in the *Ironside* episode led to guest shots in a whole flock of other shows during the next year or so, including *Marcus Welby, M.D.*, *Medical Center*, *The FBI*, *Mod Squad*, *The Survivors*, and *Bonanza!* – and finally the pilot for *The Partridge Family*.

With a popular television show, a string of hit records and a series of successful concerts to his credit, things are going beautifully at last for David Cassidy, who went from sadness to success in just a few short years. I was there for part of the journey, yet I suppose I couldn't really see it. For most of it, after all, was taking place inside his head.

But after meeting David again, I wanted to retrace that journey if I could, with David's help. I wanted to discover all it was possible to find out about David Cassidy yesterday, today, and, by learning his hopes and fears for the future, David Cassidy tomorrow.

*Chapter Two*

## DAVID'S EARLY YEARS

David Cassidy's parents. Evelyn Ward and Jack Cassidy, met when both were singing in the chorus of a Broadway musical comedy in the 1940's. After they married, they continued to work together as they kept struggling to find success in show business.

When David was born on April 12, 1950, at Flower Fifth Avenue Hospital in Manhattan, Jack and Evelyn were sharing a small Manhattan apartment in the East 20's. But with the enthusiasm of youth, they decided to announce David's birth in a typically "show business" way – by sending out announcements that read like the playbill of a Broadway show.

"EVELYN CASSIDY in association with JACK CASSIDY presents DAVID BRUCE – a new spring production," the announcements read, and listed the following credits: "Scenery by FLOWER FIFTH HOSPITAL. Costumes by LANE BRYANT. Sound Effects: EVELYN WARD. Production Asst.: JACK CASSIDY. Directed by DR. A. KINSEY. Production under supervision of DR. LOJZEAUX JR. Adapted from an original idea by ADAM. WORLD PREMIERE – APRIL 12, 1950."

Perhaps because his parents found it necessary to travel a great deal in pursuing their chosen profession – or because they realized that his grandparents, Mr. and Mrs. Fred Ward, could provide David with a better home than they could yet afford – David spent much of his first three years living with his grandparents in New Jersey.

So it was not until he was three that David lived regularly with his own parents. And though he loved his grandparents dearly, it was hardly the ideal way for a child to spend his first three formative years.

Then came the only two years in his life when David lived full-time with his own parents: the years from three to five. The Jack Cassidys made their home in Rutherford, N.J., and these were happy times for the small boy.

Jack's career had taken a sharp swing upward to stardom when he landed a leading role in a hit Broadway musical comedy, *Wish You Were Here,* which featured a real swimming pool on the stage. And when David was three-and-a-half, his mother took him to see the show. You might say it was David's first "performance" before a real audience.

When Jack Cassidy walked onto the stage, a piercing shout of joy came echoing out of the balcony as David screamed: "That's my daddy!" The whole audience responded with gales of laughter. David's first appearance was a scene-stealing hit.

His father's performance in the show, coupled with David's own first taste of audience response, left a permanent impact on the boy. It's not surprising that David decided to be a singer, and later he added acting to his ambitions. Performing became a goal from which nothing could dissuade him, even though its fulfillment was many years away.

The first real audience for his singing was his mother. David would crawl into her bed in the middle of the night, wake her up, and sing her to sleep, she recalled later. It was then that she first began to wonder if he might become a singing star like his father.

While the Jack Cassidys lived their all-too-few years together as a family, big things were happening to a girl named Shirley Jones from Smithton, Pennsylvania.

In the summer of 1953, when David was three years old, Rodgers and Hammerstein selected the 15-year-old Shirley for the chorus of their long-running Broadway musical, *South Pacific,* and quietly decided to cast her in the leading role of Laurie in the wide-screen movie version of *Oklahoma!* which would go into production the following year.

At that time, Jack Cassidy had never heard of Shirley

Jones. But after she had shot to film stardom in *Oklahoma!*, she and Jack were chosen to play the leads in a State Department tour of the same show which was to play in Paris and Rome and other cities inEurope .

By that time it was 1955, and the family life of the Jack Cassidys was coming to an end. For the Cassidy's marriage had fallen apart, and Jack Cassidy soon fell in love with Shirley Jones. David would never again live with both his parents at the same time. Evelyn and Jack were divorced in 1956 and Evelyn was given custody of their son.

Jack Cassidy, in the years ahead, would frequently be touring in some musical comedy, or traveling the night club circuit in an act with Shirley Jones, and thousands of miles might separate father and son.

Since Evelyn Ward was still working as a singer, David found himself staying once again with his grandparents from the ages of six to ten.

Shirley and Jack made their home in California after their marriage, for Shirley's film career was there and Jack could do television in Hollywood. David visited them for the summer when he was eight years old, and again when he was nine.

Then, when he was ten, David and his mother moved out to California to live, so he was able to see his dad on weekends -- when Cassidy was not touring or doing a play on Broadway.

Not long ago, Jack Cassidy was hosting *The Merv Griffin Show* on CBS Television one night. Among his guests was David, who had only recently achieved stardom on television and records.

Playing interviewer, Jack asked David if his parents' divorce had particularly hurt him

And David quietly replied that it had -- because he hadn't been able to see his father as often as he would have liked.

Suddenly the interviewing game had turned all too serious, and the television audience knew that it had been let in on a very private moment.

## Chapter Three

## AN EYE OPERATION ... AND BLINDNESS

When David Cassidy was 12 years old, suddenly his father became more than just a "weekend father" to him. He had taken David on a vacation to Hawaii, and, for a change, they could be together day after day. It was one of the happiest times in David's life.

But only a few days after their return to California, David lay in a bed at Beverly Hills Doctors Hospital, his eyes swathed in bandages following a delicate operation, and Hawaii was very far away as he longed for the moment when he would be able to see once again.

Through the mental haze caused by the pain-killing drugs, one thought prevailed: "I *will* see! And my eyes will be normal – for the first time in my life."

After all, they had promised him that he would be able to see one day soon. The doctor had promised him, and so had David's mother, that the blindness caused by his corrective eye surgery would be only temporary. And he could trust those promises – he knew he could.

He *had* to trust them. For at the moment he was completely blind.

And yet David wondered – had he made a mistake in permitting the doctor to go ahead and operate on his eyes? After all, both Dr. Cogan, who had performed the operation, and his mother had left the decision up to him, and it was David who had finally given the go-ahead. For Dr. Cogan had been treating David's eye condition for years, and David had always trusted his opinion.

David had been born with deformed muscles in both eyes. As a result, the weakened muscles did not keep his eyes in

29

proper alignment. The right eye in particular had given him trouble since the age of two.

This eye tended to be slightly "crossed." And to correct the condition, and the weakness in the other eye as well, many remedies were tried during David's childhood.

Medication was applied. David was given eye exercises to do. For a couple of years he even wore big, horn-rimmed glasses to force the eye muscles to straighten themselves. And three or four times a week for several years, David had been going to Dr. Cogan's office for special treatments.

Sometimes his eyes would appear to be getting better. And then, just as it seemed that the eye problem was about to disappear, the muscles would weaken again and his eyes would once more go slightly askew.

David found this so embarrassing that his congenital shyness was greatly increased. He hated to look in the mirror and see his slightly crossed eye. It made him feel ridiculous, at a time when he wanted most of all to be like everyone else. He wanted to be one of the gang, but secretly he was afraid that people might be laughing at him behind his back.

David's mother was equally upset about his eye problem. For she knew that it was embarrassing to him, and she also knew that it was not healthy for him to go through life with even this slight deformity, which was harmful to his vision and to his reading ability.

One day, when Evelyn had taken David to a specialist's office, the doctor told her that David was not responding to treatment as well as he should. But he told her he was sure that an eye operation would correct the problem, and assured her that it was a type of surgery which, while rather complicated, was not at all unusual.

Here it was, the chance his mother had been waiting for: the chance for David to have normal eyes at last. But although the doctor saw little risk in the operation, it was obvious to her that in such a delicate type of surgery there was always a chance of something going wrong. That was why she felt that the final decision should be up to David.

He had been waiting in another room while Evelyn and the doctor had their discussion. Now he was called in and the situation was explained to him. The doctor said it was not vital that he have the operation right away – though later on, if things got no better, it might be required. And the doctor felt it would be best to go ahead now. For David's condition was not improving at all.

The harsh truth about his eyes made David wince a little. But he pulled himself together and tried to think things through as best he could.

It was a big decision for a 12-year-old boy, but David realised that it would have to be. And so he agreed to the operation, and tried to have faith that things would go well.

Yet there was one disturbing thing that the doctor told him that day about the surgery. It would leave him temporarily blind, until the delicate eyes had healed sufficiently to distinguish light and objects once again. It might take some weeks before he could see.

To be blind, even temporarily, was a frightening prospect. To have to keep faith that you would see once again, when at the moment you could *not* see – that was a true test of faith in his doctor's ability, and faith in God's protection. But David was determined to go through with it.

His mother did what she could to reassure him. She told him she would be at his side when he woke up after the surgery. She told him again and again that everything would be all right. And David solemnly assured her that he wouldn't worry.

He did manage to enjoy the trip to Hawaii with his father, despite the operation he would face on his return. The trip meant a lot to him. It showed him that his father, despite the fact that they sometimes didn't see each other for months on end, still cared for him. It showed him that the new family his dad had started with his second wife, Shirley Jones, had not made him forget his firstborn son.

31

David enjoyed the sun and the sea in Hawaii, the cloud-covered mountains, the brilliantly colored flowers and the towering palm trees. It reminded him of California, so he felt at home there, and yet the atmosphere was different – more tropical and exotic. And he loved the friendly Hawaiian people.

But most of all he enjoyed just being with his father, seeing him every day, the way he had in the early years of his childhood, before the divorce. Each day of his vacation was treasured, and its memories stored up for the future.

But the day came when he had to fly back to California and face the operation and the long weeks of convalescence that would follow. His father could not go to the hospital with him, but promised to see him later, and to keep in touch.

David was unusually quiet on that day in late summer when his mother drove him to Beverly Hills Doctors Hospital on the corner of Beverly Glen Boulevard and Santa Monica Boulevard. The hospital, a biege, three-story structure hard by the Southern Pacific Railroad tracks, looked grim and forbidding to David as the car drove up to it.

The only touch of color was provided by several tall palm trees that grew in the forecourt of the hospital, and a few tropical flowers at their base. They were birds of paradise – the same flowers that bloomed in such profusion all over Hawaii. But Hawaii seemed awfully far away now.

David and his mother left their car and walked into the paneled first-floor lobby of the small hospital. David's mother gave their names to the receptionist, and soon they went into a small room to fill out papers pertaining to his hospitalization.

Then they were taken to David's room and, too soon for David, it was time to say their farewells. But Evelyn reassured her son that she would be back before the operation the next day, and would be with him until it was time for him to be taken to the operating room, and immediately after his surgery.

True to her word, Evelyn was there early the next morning to reassure David once again that everything would be all right. She also reminded him that he would not be able to see at first following the operation, but that it was all a normal part of the procedure. She kept stressing this so he would not panic.

David's mind was hazy now from the sedatives they had given him. But he assured Evelyn that he understood. And then, as his mother watched with an encouraging smile, David was wheeled toward the operating room.

The doctor had told Evelyn that the operation would require about two hours. But as she sat nervously in the hospital waiting room, or took a short walk to try to relax, the minutes ticked away until they had passed the two-hour mark.

She began to worry if something had gone wrong. As the hours passed, her worry increased.

At last, after five hours that seemed like five centuries, the doctor was standing in front of her, a reassuring smile on his face.

He told her that everything was fine. The operation had been a success. Then he explained why it had taken so long.

He had discovered during surgery why David's eye muscle would improve only so much and then stop. David had been born with a vein in his right eye looped around the muscle, so that when the muscle was strengthened to a certain point the vein would tend to pull it back, causing the eye to turn in again.

Only David's continued exercises had permitted the eye to correct itself temporarily even to that point, but complete and permanent correction of the condition had required surgery.

The muscle had been cut, released from the constricting

vessel, and then sewn back together again so that it could do its work unimpeded. Other minor corrections had also been made. When he had recovered from the operation in a few weeks, David would see perfectly for the first time in his life, and his eyes would no longer tend to cross.

Relieved that everything had turned out well, Evelyn thanked the doctor for his painstaking work.

When David awoke several hours later in his hospital bed, he slowly began to realize where he was. And then he remembered the brightly lighted operating room where he had fallen asleep under the anesthetic. Everything was black now. How had the operation turned out? He had to know.

His mother had promised to be there when he woke up. Was she at his side now? Softly David mumbled: "Mom ... are you ... here?" He was still groggy from the anesthetic.

Quickly his mother answered: "I'm here, David. It's all right.

And then, as he instinctively tried to open his eyes, there was no response from the eyes at all. It was as though he *had* no eyes – as though they didn't even exist. He couldn't feel anything where his eyes were supposed to be.

He cried out in fear: "I can't see!"

Quickly his mother leaned forward, took his hand, and soothingly reminded him that the doctor had said it would be that way at first. "But don't worry, you'll see again," she reassured him. "The operation was a complete success. Your eyes will be perfect when they take the bandages off."

He reached up and felt his head. It was swathed in bandages. His face was covered, except for his nostrils and mouth. He was startled. It was all so strange. . . .

What now? Just to wait. To wait in darkness for days or weeks – he didn't know exactly how long. But it did no good to think of that.

Something else was on his mind as he lay bandaged in his

34

hospital bed. He would be entering the seventh grade at Emerson Junior High School in Westwood in just a few weeks, and he wondered what it would be like, going to a new school. Some of his old friends from elementary school would be there, but mostly it would be all strangers in a big, strange school.

He hoped he would like Amerson ... and that his new classmates would like *him.*

But first he had to recover from his operation. And he was grateful that his mother was at his side to cheer him up. That day they talked until David, still feeling the effects of the anesthetic and terribly weary after all he had been through, finally lay his head back on the propped-up pillows and went to sleep. Only then did Evelyn go home.

As David lay in his hospital bed during the next several days, surrounded by darkness, listening to the radio when there was nobody there to visit him, gradually the feeling began to return to his eyes – and the feeling was one of intense pain from the surgery.

Knowing this would occur, the doctor had left instructions that David be given constant medication to lessen the pain and to help him sleep. So nearly a week passed before David was fully conscious.

This turned out to be a blessing, for it kept David from thinking too much about the fact that he could not see.

Recently, in telling me about his operation and the long days and nights that followed it, David recalled: "I was so incoherent that it didn't bother me too much. They really had me drugged up!"

And in any case, as he pointed out, "After the shock of an operation, it takes you a while to come around."

A week or so after the operation, David returned home in his mother's car, his eyes still heavily bandaged. Evelyn led him up the steps and through the front door of their house on a quiet residential street – much quieter than the noisy intersection where the hospital was located. David could notice the difference, for his ears had become more sensitive than ever in the absence of his eyesight, instinctively seeking out clues to his surroundings.

After several more days of rest, Evelyn took David to Dr. Cogan's office, where his bandages were gently and gradually removed by the doctor. The room was dim, the curtains drawn – but the small amount of light in the room was enough to make David's eyes hurt. He could dimly make out the light, though, and that was what counted. He would see again.

Quickly Dr. Cogan reached for a pair of large wrap-around goggles whose deeply tinted glass kept out most of the painful light rays. He told David to wear the goggles for a few weeks, removing them only in the evening at first so his eyes could gradually become accustomed to the light.

David agreed to follow Dr. Cogan's instructions, and then his mother took him home.

Gradually, as the days passed, David's eyes began to feel more comfortable, and he could see clearly at last . . . more clearly than ever before, in fact, for his eyes were perfectly straight now. But it was still necessary to keep the goggles on until the eyes were more nearly normal.

This caused an unexpected problem. As David explained it to me recently, "I was going into junior high school, and it was a big thing to me. I was really kind of uptight about it.

"And I had to wear those goggles! I was afraid that if I walked into the school, a new kid, wearing the goggles, it would be embarrassing.

"My mother also felt it would be a bad way for me to start off in a new school. So I didn't go to school for the first two weeks of classes. But finally I was able to leave the goggles off, and then I started school."

At Emerson Junior High School, David found himself in a whole new world . . . a world of young people beginning their first tentative steps toward adulthood. The work was harder than it had ever been before. The discipline was still strict. But he met many new friends, including some very

36

pretty girls. Somehow girls seemed more important than ever now, and he was glad he didn't have to be embarrassed about his eyes anymore.

He enjoyed being with his old friends, too. And to them, David looked subtly different. His eyes no longer had that odd look about them. In fact, they were beautiful – large, round, hazel eyes, thickly fringed with brown lashes. Girls who hadn't given him a second look in elementary school suddenly began to take notice.

Less than a decade later, David Cassidy's eyes would cause girls' hearts all over the country to beat a little faster. His eyes would be considered the best feature of his handsome face.

But few who would look at those beautiful eyes so admiringly would realize the pain and fear that David Cassidy had undergone in order to make their vision and their appearance normal.

David himself will never forget the special fears that he summer of 1962 ... the fears that only blindness can bring.

But it was all well worth it. And today, as David Cassidy views the world with shining eyes and unclouded vision, he may well breathe a silent prayer of thanks for the skillful surgeon who made it all possible ... the loyal mother who was there when David needed her ... and, perhaps, for his own courage in agreeing to the operation that changed his life.

## Chapter Four

## "I WENT TO SCHOOL WITH DAVID CASSIDY"

Among the new friends David Cassidy met at Emerson Junior High School in the fall of 1962 was a boy named Duncan Lent, who still remembers their friendship very well.

The picture he paints of David is that of a very average boy, one of the gang – certainly not a boy who seemed destined for stardom as a teenage idol. His view of David seems to be the same one that his other friends had at that time.

"I first met Dave in front of the Village Delicatessen, where a lot of us from Emerson used to hang around in those days," Duncan told me recently. The Village Deli is right next to the Fox Village Theatre, and the theatre's large courtyard is a pleasant place, with plants and shrubbery that gave it a village square atmosphere.

"When I came into the seventh grade," Duncan remembers, "it meant a change of schools, and I met a lot of new people. Dave and I became part of the same clique, I guess you could say, along with Alex MacDonald, through whom you met him. There were several of us kids – boys and girls – who began running around together and going to the same parties.

"David was never in the limelight or anything. In fact, he was kind of on the outskirts of our little group. He wasn't the center of attention or anything like that. In fact, nobody really paid *any* attention to him.

"Although he was in our group, he was the kind of guy who seemed as though he would have a few close personal friends, rather than a lot of casual acquaintances," Duncan recalls.

39

"What was your first impression of David?" I asked him.

"My first impression? That he was a nice guy. In fact, I always did like the guy. He was friendly. I had no idea that he was interested in singing or acting. He never mentioned it to me. He just seemed like a regular guy, like anyone else in the group.

"I became good friends with him for a while," Duncan remembers, "until I moved away from Los Angeles. I spent the night at his house a few times – the house in Cheviot Hills, which was near a golf course. I met his mother there at the house and thought she was very nice.

"Dave also used to go over and visit his dad, Jack Cassidy, and his stepmother, Shirley Jones, at their house. I knew that Jack Cassidy was a star in show business, and I thought Shirley Jones was really beautiful. I remember my father liked her a lot from seeing her in the movies. So I always knew that David came from a show-business background."

"How did David get along with Shirley in those days?" I asked Duncan.

"He got along with her fine! He never said anything against her – never complained. He liked her," Duncan remembered.

"What sort of things did you and David and your friends do to pass the time?" I asked.

"Nothing, almost!" Duncan laughed. "We never had any hobbies or anything. We just hung around the delicatessen and went around Westwood together or visited each other's houses. Sometimes we went to parties.

"David showed no special interest in music that I can remember," he added. "I don't even remember listening to records at his house."

"How were his grades?" I asked. "Was he very good in school?"

"I don't think so. He was just kind of a goof-off, like everybody else at that age!" Duncan said with a grin. "At that age," he explained, "it's just kind of a social trip, when you've come into a new world. That was when we first really started noticing the chicks and hanging around with them, and going to parties."

"How did the girls treat David?" I wondered.

"Nicely. He was just kind of quiet, you know? It wasn't really a dating situation yet, anyway. It was just a case of hanging around with your own clique.

"I don't think Dave had any girl friends when we were in the seventh grade. Boys and girls would all go around together in groups, and we'd go to parties that way, too," Duncan remembered.

"What do you think of Dave's success today?" I asked him.

"It really flashed me!" he admitted. "I was in Hawaii, where I live now, and I was watching *The Partridge Family*, which I had never seen before. That was when I saw him on television for the first time. And I said, 'I used to know that guy!'

"It just seemed like a natural thing for him to do, actually, since his family is in show business. But I was surprised nevertheless – since, as I said, I never knew that he was an actor, or that he even wanted to be.

"But then," Duncan added, "I knew Dave at an age when all we had on our minds was meeting girls and going to parties. Nobody was really interested in anything else. . . ."

## Chapter Five

## NOT EXACTLY AN ANGEL

One old friend of David Cassidy's who was not surprised by his amazing success is Alex MacDonald, the boy who first introduced him to me in 1963.

For Alex, who has since moved away from California, was back briefly in 1969 and visited David at his home, at a time when Dave was just beginning his television career.

"Dave was already working hard at his career the last time I saw him," Alex recalls. "He had already done his first television show, *Ironside*, and was negotiating to appear on *Bonanza!* at the time." He had been in a Broadway play, had a manager, Ruth Aarons, and was really doing well. But he was as nice as ever, Alex discovered.

"If he was working so hard then, I can imagine what it must be like for him now," Alex added. "I'd sure like to see him again, though, if he has the time." (We were talking by long-distance telephone, and Alex had not been in California for some time, since he now lives in the South.)

When I told him that David always makes time to see his old friends – indeed, that his best friends are still the ones he knew in school – Alex sounded very happy to hear it. But he knows that things will never be the same as they were in the old, carefree days, when he and David were not only the best of friends, but the worst of mischief-makers.

Alex MacDonald knows better than anyone that Dave Cassidy was not exactly an angel when he was in his early teens. They met just after David had turned 13, when Alex entered Emerson Junior High School at the beginning of the second semester early in 1963. David had already been there for one semester, and he quickly showed Alex the ropes.

"We had a couple of classes together, even though I was a year younger and a semester behind him," Alex recalls. "We didn't like our history teacher, and we used to throw spitballs at her."

He suddenly corrected himself. "No – we used to throw Red Hots at her! That's what it was. You know, those little pieces of red candy. We got thrown out of her class a couple of times for that."

As the memories of schoolboy mischief started coming back, Alex took obvious delight in them.

"We were in M.P. together. I don't remember anymore what that stands for. But it's a special home room they put students in when they don't make good grades.

"And we were in S.A. together – that's Special Adjustment," he added. "That's where you go if you get in trouble on the lunch grounds."

Although David made poor grades sometimes, he hated to let his parents find out, just as any boy would. And he did what many others had done before him. "I don't know if I should tell you this, but I remember the time when Dave and I forged our report cards," Alex confessed.

"We forged them all straight A's," he said, a mischievous laugh in his voice. "When Dave's parents saw his all-A report card, they gave him a bunch of presents, including a surfboard and a minibike.

"And then, when they found out somehow that his report card had been forged, and that his real grades were D's and F's, they took all the presents back!"

Alex paused, perplexed. "I *still* don't know how they managed to find out...."

"Did you ever stay at Dave's house?" I asked him.

"Oh, yeah – all the time!"

"What was it like when you visited him?"

"I'll tell you. One night we sneaked one of our friends into his house, and the guy slept all night in the closet in Dave's room, so that Dave's parents wouldn't notice him."

44

"Why didn't his parents want the other boy there?" I wondered.

"I don't know. I don't think Dave ever asked them for permission. We just smuggled him in for the heck of it!" Alex replied.

"What else did you do when you visited?" I asked – almost afraid to by that time.

"We'd go out and throw eggs at cars," Alex recalled. Then he corrected himself. "No, it wasn't eggs. It was eggs with flour inside.

"We'd take the yolks out first, through a little hole, and then we'd put the flour inside through the same hole. Dave showed me how to do it. I'd never done it before."

Remembering those long-ago schoolboy pranks, Alex sighed wistfully. "Yes, Dave was a great guy! He was my best friend."

"Since you were the best of friends, did he ever tell you anything about wanting to go into show business?" I wondered.

"No," Alex said firmly. "He never had any idea *what* he wanted to do for a career, as far as I knew at that time."

"Didn't you know that he'd already been in summer stock with his mother by then?" I asked.

He seemed very surprised to hear this. "In summer stock? *That* young? No, he never talked about it. I guess maybe he was ashamed to admit it, or something."

Apparently David feared that he wouldn't be looked on as a "regular guy" by others of his age if he admitted having sung in summer stock. And at that stage in his life, it was very important to him to be accepted by his contemporaries.

Alex also remembers other less mischievous moments that he spent with David, some of them fairly recent.

"We used to ride our bikes together around Century City. I remember Dave always wore that blue parka of his when the weather was cool.

"And then, the last time I saw him, after he had appeared

45

in *Ironside*, we used to listen to records – although we didn't do that in the days when we were in junior high school. The last I knew, he was really into B.B. King. That was his favorite record artist. He was still living in the house on Glenbar in Cheviot Hills with his mother, who's a very nice lady. He still hadn't moved out at that time, in the fall of 1969, although he had been in New York for awhile studying singing and doing the Broadway play.

"So I wasn't surprised when he became so successful, since he was already doing so well on television the last time I saw him," Alex noted.

"What do you think of his television show, *The Partridge Family*?" I asked him.

"I haven't even seen him on TV yet," Alex admitted. "But I hear it's a good show, and I think that's terrific.

"Yes, I'm sure glad for Dave," his old friend said warmly. "I hope he makes a lot of money. He deserves it. He's a nice guy!"

*Chapter Six*

## DAVID'S BITTERSWEET
## INTERRACIAL ROMANCE

The American spring of 1968 was a time of assassinations, as Martin Luther King and Robert F. Kennedy were felled by gunmen's bullets. And their deaths would touch David Cassidy personally.

But for a while at least, while these men still lived, that spring was a time of hope for many young people. And for 18-year-old David, it was a time of discovery and romance.

He had changed a great deal since his carefree, mischievous junior high school days, and had said goodbye to some of his good friends. Both Duncan Lent and Alex MacDonald had moved away from Los Angeles. But he still saw a good deal of Sam Hyman, another friend from Emerson Junior High, who would become his roommate one day and share the excitement of his sudden stardom.

His sophomore and junior years in high school were over, too – the years at University High and Hamilton High – and with them, the unhappiness he had felt at 16 and 17, when his mother's marriage to his stepfather broke up and he himself was prevented from seeking a show business career.

He had spent the summer between his junior and senior years appearing in plays with the Los Angeles Theatre Company, and during his senior year at Rexford he knew that upon graduation he would be able to pursue his career in earnest.

So David was content to spend his senior year enjoying high school and the new friends he met at Rexford, as well as the trusted friends he still retained from the past.

47

He had a girl friend now, and he was happy. Had he known how short a time his happiness would last, he might have treasured it all the more – might even have fought harder to hold on to it. For, looking back later, he would realize that the end of that springtime romance was at least partially his fault.

At any rate, David was cheerful and optimistic as that crucial spring of 1968 began, not knowing that it would leave him changed, older – and a little sadder. For he had a girl of his own, and that was all that mattered at the moment.

Since he had always been free of racial prejudice, the fact that the girl was black really made no difference to David. He couldn't know that later it *would* make a difference – to her.

And yet, if Robert Kennedy had not died – and especially if Martin Luther King had not died – things might have been very different for David and the girl.

Still, David has his memories of her, and of the few short months they were together. Recently he agreed to share his memories with me . . . and with you.

"I met her at Rexford School during my senior year," David recalled, as we sat on a grassy lawn at the Screen Gems ranch between takes on his ABC-TV series, *The Partridge Family*. The multicolored Partridge Family bus was nearby, with the family's musical instruments on top of it for a scene. The technicians were busily setting up another shot.

But David didn't notice them. His voice was soft and almost hesitant as he turned his thoughts to the past, to that last year when he was still just David Cassidy, a private person, rather than David Cassidy, the actor, the singer, and eventually, the star.

"She was a student at Rexford, one of my classmates. She lived in South Los Angeles, and I never knew how she got the bread to go to Rexford, because she wasn't wealthy at

48

all. And Rexford was fairly expensive," David remembered.

Indeed it was expensive. Rexford is a private junior and senior high school, and among David's classmates was Dino Martin. That's the kind of school it is.

"I think her mother had put money away for her, and her father had, too. She lived with her mother, and she was going to Rexford with a girl friend of hers who was also from South Los Angeles. Her girl friend was black, too. They had a long way . . . a *long* way . . . to come to school every day."

It was a long way in more ways than one. South Los Angeles is a largely Negro area. Watts is in that general part of town. The schools there could not compare to Rexford. The wages people earned there could not compare with the salaries of the Beverly Hills, Bel Air and West Los Angeles parents who sent their children to Rexford. The life there could not compare with the life David Cassidy, Dino Martin and their friends had known, even though Dino was far wealthier than David.

It was, in truth, another world – and a journey from there to Rexford School on Pico Boulevard in West Los Angeles was indeed a long, long way.

But the girl had somehow made it. at who knows what sacrifice on the part of her parents. And now there she was, and when David Cassidy first saw her his heart stopped.

"She was really a . . . really a beautiful lady," he said slowly. "She just was *fantastic* looking. And she was bright! And, you know, she laughed a lot. She was pleasant. She didn't appear to be bitter at all."

He stopped, as if the next words were hard to say. "And she was *already* bitter!"

But David didn't know that – not when he first met her. Only later did he learn it, when the bitterness increased until it finally burst its way through the surface of her pleasant personality to reveal the hidden depths of suffering below.

49

"After I met her," David said as he continued his story, "it took me about six months, really, to get in that close with her where I felt secure enough to ask her out.

"And then I went to a party with her. It was an all-black party, and she just made me feel really good. I don't know . . . I just liked her a lot."

"Did the other black people at the party accept you?" I asked him.

"Yes – to some extent. I don't think they were that hung up about it," David replied. "It was a time when Bobby Kennedy was out here campaigning, so they were all into that. They were all campaigning, and so was she. I wasn't really into campaigning for any of the candidates, but I just wanted to go with her.

"Actually it was a party, I think, for *him* – for Bobby Kennedy – or something similar to that. He wasn't there at the time, however. I think he had been earlier.

"There were around a hundred people there, and they were all black. So I felt very strange, because the usual situation was reversed. You see, I'd been in a situation where there were all white people and only one black person, but this was a new experience for me.

"I felt a little uncomfortable," David admitted, "and at the same time I felt *very* comfortable being where I was. I mean, the fact that I was the one person there who was white, and yet was accepted, made me feel really good."

After that, David dated the girl, "for maybe four months," he estimated.

"How did your folks feel about it?" I asked him.

"My parents were 'white liberals,' " he said. He added with a grin, "They always told me, 'Yellow, red and black and white, you're all precious in His sight.'' Prejudice was never inbred in me – but I always knew the difference. I knew which one was black and which one was white."

"Is that why it took you so long to ask her out?" I wondered.

"Well, only because I didn't know what *her* reaction to it

would be. Until I was sure that she would really be in favor of it, I didn't want to ask her or offend her, or blow my scene with her already. Because I was good friends with her."

"How did *her* parents react to you?" I asked.

"Well, they were on the same kind of trip I was, you know? Because she had never gone out with a white guy before, either. And it was really strange. But they weren't against me."

Where did David and the girl go on their dates? "Friends' houses, movies . . . I saw a lot of films in those days."

He smiled as he remembered something. "I saw *Guess Who's Coming to Dinner* with her. Wow! It was a *trip*. I went with her, and Sam Hyman, who's now my roommate, went with his girl friend. We went on a double date. It was fun!"

"Some people," I observed, "feel that *Guess Who's Coming to Dinner* is a phony movie." (I was referring to the commonly-noted fact that when Hollywood finally showed a white girl in love with a black man he had to be the idealized, super-perfect type so often played by Sidney Poitier.) "Did she comment on it?"

"Well, I don't know. . . . I wasn't really into the movie yet that much. I mean – yeah, there was a lot of *shuck* in that movie," he said, using a descriptive word that I had never heard before. "*You* know – come *on*! Sidney Poitier being the Negro? Give me a break!"

David continued, using the youthful jargon of his contemporaries as he told me what broke up his romance with the black girl. "Eventually, I got pretty bum-tripped by her. You see, what really sort of broke us up is the fact that she got involved with a guy who went to Harvard. He was black. He was really bright, and very into the college situation and the scene. He was very 'black power' at the time, and just then black power was reaching its height.

"Martin Luther King had just been killed. I remember going down to her house the night he was killed. And I was

51

just so paranoid – I can't *tell* you how paranoid I was!

"It was around Watts, and I was white and I was young, and I had long hair. And I was driving in a fairly nice car. I was really paranoid as I drove around, driving down to pick her up. Maybe I'm overdramatizing a bit, but. . . ."

But it was clear that David had indeed been frightened that evening, an evening when much of Washington was ablaze with rioting over King's death. And perhaps David had some inkling of what would happen later to his romance.

Yet as far as the girl herself was concerned, everything seemed fine between them. "When I saw her that night, she and I were really together," David recalled. "She didn't blame me for what had happened."

But could Martin Luther King's death have affected her thoughts about David later? "Yes, I think the whole thing . . . this guy from Harvard really brainwashed her. As I said before, the reason that we sort of broke up is because she started seeing him.

"And I don't know, I just . . . I was pretty immature at the time, I suppose, and I was paying less attention to her, maybe, because of that, rather than trying to win her back. I just sort of ignored her because of that, and I guess that made her just turn to him all the more."

"You mean you felt hurt?" I asked.

"Yeah, right! And so I said, 'Well, she can do *that*, so I can do *this*.' Also, she thought I really dug her girl friend, the one she used to come to school with, because I was friendly with the girl friend, too."

Then David confessed, "Maybe I played that up a little more than I should have, because I wanted to make her a bit jealous. . . ."

He paused. "And then she became very, very radical – like, that fast! In fact, the only thing that really crunched it was something she said in school one day. . . ."

The class was having a discussion about race riots, "because it was really a progressive school, at least compared to public schools," David recalls. "We were rapping, and I remember my friend Kevin also was talking about it. Really, it was Kevin and me against her, kind of, in the discussion.

"And I also had another thing going. I mean, we were having a class discussion, but in reality we were discussing her and me – the situation between us," David explained.

"I asked her, 'If there was a riot ... and I was running down the street ... and you saw five black guys coming after me ... and I said, 'It's me!' and I ran into your house ... what would you do?'"

"She said, 'I'd shoot you!'

"And I said, 'Okay – got your ticket, baby.'"

That was how it ended for them – suddenly and publicly, with those frightening words of hers. After that, any close relationship between David and the black girl seemed impossible at the time.

And yet, after he had finished telling me the story of his broken romance with the beautiful black girl, David added suddenly: "I'd like to see her now. I don't know where she is, though. ..."

So the years haven't dimmed his memories of this girl to whom he was once so close. He can't forget all the good things they shared, before the world closed in on them. And with the wisdom of increased maturity, he thinks he understands a little better some of the hurt and humiliation she must have suffered in her own difficult life, which made her finally say what she did. So if he and the girl ever met again, David hopes they can be friends.

Perhaps that will be possible if the girl reads this. For although David never used her name in telling me the story, *she* knows who she is.

Some will feel that this story of David Cassidy's interracial romance should not have been told at all. Others will insist that it had to be told just as it happened. I felt that it should be made known, if only because it tells something about what David Cassidy is today – why he wants to help and understand other people, lest hatred and prejudice be allowed to destroy the world. It tells, too, how things have been these past few years for all of us.

Perhaps tomorrow the world will be different. But this story happened yesterday.

## Chapter Seven

## THE TRAGEDY
## DAVID CAN'T FORGET

Although David Cassidy has fond memories of many friends he knew in junior and senior high school and wants to renew acquaintances with some he has not seen lately, it hurts him to this day to think about the death of a boy who was at one time his best friend: a boy named Kevin.

And the memory also brings pain to Judy Strangis, the beautiful young actress whom David has dated.

For Judy, who has given many fine performances as Helen on *Room 222*, the popular ABC-TV series, was Kevin's girl friend. In fact it was Kevin who first introduced her to David, years before David won stardom on *The Partridge Family*.

Judy and David share a tragic secret. For they know that but for a twist of fate it might have been David who died instead of Kevin.

Both David and Kevin belonged to a generation that lost some of its finest members to drugs. Both ran with the same crowd. Both faced the same deadly temptations. These killed Kevin, while David survived.

Yet, but for this unkind fate, Kevin might be a star today like David. Indeed, they might have become roommates in David's beautiful house.

Kevin's story also brings great sadness to me personally, as well as to David. For I met him when he was one of the crowd David ran around with in Westwood during David's schooldays. He worked at a store close to my apartment, and I remember seeing him there many times. He was a friendly boy and a good worker.

Yet, although Kevin's story is a tragic one, I think he

55

would want it told – not only to warn other youngsters away from the drugs that eventually killed him, but also because he was proud of his friendship with David, and proud of David's success on television and records, which was already making him a national favorite at the time that Kevin died in November, 1970.

When Kevin was alive, he was refreshingly frank in admitting that he enjoyed sharing in David's reflected glory. And now that he is dead, I think he would have wanted his friendship with David to be remembered.

"Kevin always respected David," Judy Strangis recalled when we got together recently in Westwood to talk about her friendship with the two boys. "He was really happy about David's success. He loved it and was so glad for him. On one interview, I talked about Kevin, and he was so excited: 'You talked about *me*!' I had told how I met David through Kevin.

"They were both seniors at Rexford School in Beverly Hills when Kevin introduced me to David," Judy continued, "Kevin was working for my uncle, who owns a cleaning store, and one day Kevin took David with him to help on deliveries.

"They went to places like Andre Previn's house to deliver cleaning, driving a big van. And during the day they came by to see me.

"David and Kevin had known each other at Emerson Junior High School, but it was during their senior year at Rexford that they became super good friends.

"Kevin and I were going together at the time, and when he and I would get into an argument, David would call me and say, 'Hello, Judy. I heard you and Kevin were in an argument. Would you like to go out with me?'

"But the thing I didn't know at the time was that Kevin had him do it! He wanted to see what my reaction was – if I would go out with other people," Judy smiled.

Actually, David would help Judy and Kevin to patch up their quarrels. He had no intention of moving in on Kevin's girl. And to this day, although he and Judy have dated, they are only friends, and have never been sweethearts. In fact, David didn't really ask Judy for a date – except to test her fidelity to Kevin at his request – until after Kevin and Judy had decided not to date anymore.

"David and Kevin always seemed to have lunch at the Jack-in-the-Box hamburger stand on Pico Boulevard, near Rexford School, during their senior year," Judy remembers. "I have a sister, Cindy, who's married now. She used to be in show business, appearing with Ray Anthony's band. But at the time when David was at Rexford, Cindy was working as a part-time receptionist for a lawyer nearby.

"Since she already knew Kevin, she began eating at Jack-in-the-Box with the two of them sometimes – David and Kevin. She always liked David. And as soon as he saw her, he went ape over her! He fell in love with her on the spot.

"Cindy was several years older than David, so they never dated. But to this day he has a crush on her. It's just a harmless crush, since she's married now, but she and David are still friends. Sometimes he's seen her at my house when he and I have dated.

"Kevin and David were in the drama class at Rexford," Judy continued, "and they were both good – *very* good! Then, when David went East after he graduated from Rexford, I lost touch with him for a while.

"I didn't know he had become a professional actor until one night I was watching television and I suddenly saw him guest starring on one of those dramatic shows that he did. I was shocked! But it looked like David Cassidy – it *was* David Cassidy. I can't remember which show he was on, *Marcus Welby, M.D.*, or *Medical Center*. I know he did them both.

"But I do remember that a month or so later I turned on *Bonanza!* and there he was again. He did show after show. I couldn't believe it. He was great!"

Judy saw David again for the first time since his Rexford days when they met at an ABC network party in June,

1970. By that time Judy was no longer dating Kevin. She was already on *Room 222*, and David was filming *The Partridge Family* for airing in the fall.

"It was at the Bistro in Beverly Hills," Judy recalls. "David saw me, and I saw him. I wasn't going to say anything, because we hadn't seen each other in over a year and I didn't think he remembered me.

"But all of a sudden he went, 'Judy!' and I went, 'David!' He was with Susan Dey, and I thought she was his date. I didn't know that they were in *The Partridge Family* together.

"David asked, 'Do you mind if I call you?' and I said, 'Not at all!' So he wrote my phone number on his hand, and I didn't think he'd remember it.

"But about a month later he called me. He said he had seen me on some television show. And he asked, 'How would you like to go out to a publicity party for Bell Records with me?' I said, 'Fine,' and we went to it. That was in August."

"I saw you there with David," I told Judy. "That was the first time I had seen him since the days when I used to know him in Westwood, when he was in junior high school." And Judy remembered that we had met.

"He was so nervous at the party!" she said. "In fact, the whole time he said to me, 'Just hold onto me. Hold onto me!' Because it was before his first record had come out, and he was very, very nervous. But he handled it very well."

That was how Judy's dates with David began. But a month or so later, they almost ended.

"In September I was on television three times in one week," Judy recalls. "One Wednesday I was on *Room 222*, an hour later I was on *Dan August*, and that Friday night I was a guest star on *Love American Style*. That was the same night David was premiering on *The Partridge Family*.

"Just after I was on *Dan August* that Wednesday, I got a phone call. It was David. I hadn't talked to him for a while,

58

and he said, 'I just saw you on television and I really liked you – and I want to get together with you.'

"So I said, 'Fine.' I was busy the next night, Thursday, so I asked, 'What about Friday?'

"David said, 'Well, I'm on television Fridays.' And I said, 'I'm on, too. You're on at 8:30, and I'm on at 10 on *Love American Style.*'

"He told me, 'Well, I've got to go over to Shirley's (David's stepmother, Shirley Jones) house and watch the show. And then after the show I'll come by, and we'll watch your *Love American Style* together.'

"Well, something happened and my phone got disconnected," Judy told me sadly. "It was out of order that Friday evening. So I waited, and *Love American Style* was on, and David didn't come over and I didn't hear from him.

"So after my show was over, I waited a few minutes, and then I thought, 'Oh, forget it! He's not going to come.' And I went to bed.

"A half hour later there was a knock on the door, and my mom answered. It was David. He got tied up, and my phone was out of order, so he couldn't call me.

"My mom said, 'Well, gee, David, she's asleep.' So he got really upset, and he left. And he didn't talk to me after that, because of what I did. He thought I had stood him up.

"I *didn't* stand him up. It's just that I didn't know my phone was out of order, so I didn't think he was coming over," Judy said.

She paused, and then added slowly, "We didn't talk for a long time after that – until close to the time when Kevin died. . . ."

Judy continued, "When we did talk on the phone a few times, it was I who called David. And he seemed – a little indifferent. We didn't see each other for some time. David never mentioned what had happened that night. We both just left it up in the air."

And then came that day in November, 1970 – the day

59

when Judy called David to tell him that Kevin had died. . . .

"David wasn't at home. But his roommate, Sam, was," Judy recalls. "I had never met Sam before, and I was so hysterical on the phone that Sam could barely understand me.

"When Sam heard the news from me, he was in total shock, since he and David and Kevin had all attended Emerson Junior High together.

"I had to work on *Room 222* the day of Kevin's funeral, so I couldn't attend. I visited the funeral chapel the night before instead. But I told Sam, 'Please – if David isn't working, tell him to go.'

"Well, as it turned out, somebody had called David earlier that morning while he was sleeping, and had told him that Kevin was dead.

"So David, too, was in a state of shock. And he went to the funeral with some of his friends."

I told Judy, "When I talked to David in September, 1970, we discussed Kevin. I had heard that he was in a very depressed state, but David told me, 'Kevin's all right now.' "

"No one knows, really, what finally happened," Judy said quietly. "Nobody knows if it was a suicide, or if it was an accident.

"The only thing I know is that Kevin had a party on a Saturday night. He mixed alcohol with 'downers' – barbiturates – or something. And he O.D.'d. He just kept drinking more and more, so nobody knows if it was an accident."

Ironically, Kevin had seemingly conquered his drug habit at the time he was dating Judy. In fact, she said, during his entire senior year at Rexford – the year they were going steady – Kevin had not touched drugs.

"He was studying acting at the time," Judy recalls. "I went to his acting class with him one day, and he was great. He tried out for the Los Angeles company of *Fortune and Men's Eyes* and almost won a part. But after he didn't get it,

60

he kind of gave up. . . ." And eventually Kevin started taking drugs again, shortly after his mother died.

David, too, was trying to break into acting at just about that time. And luck and determination were on his side. For although he, like Kevin, suffered rejections at first, he kept trying, until he succeeded.

But then – David had not suffered the personal tragedies that Kevin had endured. David's parents, like Kevin's, were divorced, but both of David's folks were still living. And the death of Kevin's mother began the string of misfortunes which ended only with his own death.

Kevin's renewed use of drugs had contributed to his breakup with Judy. But the two remained good friends always. David and Kevin also maintained *their* close friendship, even though David was busy with his successful career by that time. And Judy recalls that David would talk to Kevin in an attempt to help him to straighten out his life, never realizing that his life had such a short course to run.

"David tried to help. And he told me that before he and Sam moved to their house in the Hollywood Hills, he asked Kevin to be their roommate," Judy remembers.

But those plans were never carried out. For in November, 1970, Kevin's grandfather passed away, and the very next day Kevin, perhaps unable to deal with yet another tragic loss of a loved one, might have taken his own life.

Yet although Kevin is now gone, David continues to maintain his friendships with the friends he has known since his schooldays, realizing that they have always liked him for himself, and not for his newfound fame.

"David was always nice when he was in high school. He was always mellow," says Judy approvingly. "But now that he's successful, he's as nice as ever!

"He still has the same friends he's had since school. And so do I, for that matter. I don't go to Hollywood parties, unless I have to for business reasons, and I don't think David does, either. So I don't really know David's reaction to the public – the people who wait outside parties to see celebrities," Judy noted.

"But you must have seen him being approached by fans," I replied.

"Well, no. When I go with David, we always kind of go to places where there aren't a lot of people, unless it's one of those industry functions. Even then, I've never been with him when he has been mobbed.

"During a visit to Dave Madden's beach place, we walked along the beach and kids would come up and ask for David's autograph. He'd say, 'Oh, yeah – sure!' and he would always sign willingly.

"In fact, at one point we saw a couple of kids on the beach and he walked over to them and said, 'Hi – I'm David,' and talked with them. He was really polite!"

Obviously David loves such rare opportunities to talk to one or two fans on a casual, informal basis, and actively seeks out chances to do so when he can. It's only when individuals turn into a surging crowd that he tries to escape, for the safety of all concerned.

"I recall one time when we were Dave Madden's guests for the day, one of his neighbors came over with his family and also spent the day," Judy continued.

"Well, this man's little girl had a very bad heart. And Dave Madden's house is up a long, long flight of stairs from the beach. Even if you're in good shape, you can really get out of breath climbing up and down those stairs!

"The minute David found out that this little girl had a bad heart, he told her, 'Hey! I don't want you walking down those stairs. I'll carry you down.'

"And so he carried this poor little girl down that long flight of stairs to the beach. And she was in seventh heaven because David Cassidy actually carried her down those stairs.

"In fact, she asked me, 'Judy, did *you* tell him to carry me down?' Because she had loved David for years. And I said quite truthfully, 'No! I swear I didn't say a word. It's David who thought of doing it.' I'll never forget it, because it was like 50 steps, a really long walk down, and David was beautiful about it."

Then she paused and added quietly, "Yes, there's something really nice in David that makes him do things like that for people. . . .

"I'll tell you another very nice thing that David did," Judy added. "I'm listed in the telephone book, and I have a lot of fans calling me. I get calls from all over the world – you wouldn't *believe* how many people call! Many of them ask me questions about David, of course.

"One day a little girl came over to my house with her father," Judy remembers. "And she went into my room to try to get David's phone number out of my book!

"I told her, 'Don't you *dare* go in there!' Then she begged me to call him.

"I said I didn't want to. But she kept asking and asking.

"So finally I went into my room, hid my phone book, and then called David.

"I said, 'David, I've got a little girl here. Would you please talk to her?'

"Well, David talked to her on the phone, and she was the happiest girl in the whole, wide world!

"But it's funny," Judy mused. "When the little girl was talking to me, she talked all the time. But when she was on the phone with David, she was stunned. She couldn't think of one thing to ask him!"

The little girl was not unusual in this. Many fans do everything in their power to get a chance to talk to some star they admire. And then, when the chance is theirs by some happy circumstance, they suddenly get tongue-tied and don't know what to say.

But David takes this for the compliment that it actually is, and does his best to put such fans at ease. For he knows how they feel, and sympathizes with them. And he knows it is they who have made him popular.

"Another thing that's nice about David – he's not a

phony," Judy points out. "He's the kind of person who says exactly what he feels!

"And he doesn't like to talk about show business with his friends. He's not that kind of person. He wants to talk to people about how they live and what they think. He likes to really rap and get into very deep conversations. That's the only way he feels he really knows somebody.

"If you're over at his house, he won't say to you, 'I'm doing this concert and that concert.' He doesn't get into show business talk at all at times like that.

"But as I said, he'll tell you just what he thinks. And he gets mad at me sometimes because, no matter what somebody says to me, I'm always nice. He thinks that sometimes I'm *too* nice to people!

David claims that if someone says anything that bothers me, I should tell that person how I feel. I shouldn't hold it in. He likes people who express themselves frankly.

"Even if they were to say something mean to him, David would respect them as long as they were frank," Judy notes. "They could say, 'You're being obnoxious!' or 'Who do you think you are? You think you're Mr. Conceited!' And David wouldn't get angry.

"Yes, David really takes criticism well. If somebody tells him something that he knows is for his own good, he'll not only listen – he'll take the advice.

"Because David does like people to be very honest with him," Judy noted, "He himself is completely honest with *them* – hoping that they'll be the same in return.

"For instance, David and his roommate, Sam Hyman, are *very* honest with each other. They don't hold anything back. And they have a very nice friendship because of that.

"Another thing: Sam never interferes. When David is doing something at the house that's involved with his career, something that doesn't have anything to do with Sam, then Sam will leave the house or go to another room. He doesn't try to get into the act.

"That's another reason that David and Sam get along

This is probably the first photo ever taken of David Cassidy recording. He was obviously at home with a microphone even then, in 1965. PHOTO BY JAMES GREGORY

David Cassidy at the age of 14 with his good friend, Alex MacDonald, whose reminiscences of David are included in this book. PHOTO BY JAMES GREGORY

David Cassidy with author James Gregory

David Cassidy and friend relaxing at home.

very well. Neither of them interferes in the other's private concerns, whether it's business or something personal," Judy pointed out. "Yet they do many things together, and they like to travel together, because they understand each other.

"Sam is a good person – a really nice guy," Judy said with great sincerity. "I think he's good for David. Everything has happened so fast for David, and Sam talks to him and gives him advice.

"Sam wants to get into show business, so David has had Sam help him on his concerts. Sam designed the posters for the concerts. And he's going to acting school now. His regular job has been as a film editor.

"I've been going over to their house, and we've had dinner there together," Judy noted. "Since David is often mobbed by fans when he goes out to some public place, he often entertains his friends at home instead.

"When David is at home, there's nobody to interfere in his personal life," Judy pointed out, noting, "now David lives in the San Fernando Valley.

"But basically David is a very happy person. He's proud of what he has accomplished, but he's not conceited. And his friends and family are proud of him, too."

Even the false rumors to which public personalities are often subjected don't faze David. As Judy smilingly pointed out, "I remember a time when David and I hadn't seen each other for a while, and all of a sudden he phoned me and said, 'You're not going to believe this – we're engaged!'

"Somebody had said in an article that David and I were engaged. And we hadn't even seen each other for some time when the article came out. So we laughed about the rumor!

"Yes, we have a lot of fun. And we have a lot in common," Judy said, "because David is not ready to get serious with anyone romantically, and I'm not, either. Yet I don't mind going out to industry functions with him, because I have to go to them, too.

"So it's convenient for us to go out together. If David has to go to an awards banquet, for instance, he'll say, 'Judy, can you go with me?' And I'll understand what's involved.

"I'm sure the pressure of his career gets rough sometimes. And yet I know that the fact that we have a lot of fun together and goof around helps him to relax.

"David has the busiest schedule of anybody I know," Judy marvels. "It's just unbelievable – I don't know how he does it! He has the TV show, plus recordings, concerts, and publicity layouts, so that he has no time at all to himself during the week.

"Yet he likes to entertain at home at night when he gets a chance. And when he does, there are always lots of kids over there.

"In fact, I was at his house one afternoon, and people were just walking in and out of the house without even knocking! That was when he lived in the Hollywood Hills.

"On weekends, though, David likes to get away to the beach whenever he can, just to rest and think," Judy pointed out.

Although Judy and David are just good friends, she admits with a mischievous smile that "I've always had a crush on David. I used to kid Kevin when we were going together by telling him about my crush.

"It was always a joke, but Kevin used to get jealous. For he really thought that I liked David, because when I would talk to David on the phone, I would get excited.

"But I was very careful of what I said to David. The first thing I ever said to him was, 'David, you're an Aries. I've got to stay away!' Because, you see, I always really like Aries people.

"But one thing about me that always discouraged David is the fact that I'm from a very strict Catholic family, and Kevin would always tell David that I couldn't do this and I couldn't do that, how I had a curfew, and how strict my family was.

"In fact, David said recently that he even used to be afraid to hold my hand because I was such a respectable girl. And to this day, he'll try never to use any swear words in front of me," Judy notes. "And if he does, he'll always say, 'Oh, Judy, I'm really sorry. Please excuse me!'

"And then he'll admit, 'I've got this mental thing about you in my head. I always remember what Kevin said.' That's why we both have a lot of respect for each other."

Yes, David Cassidy always remembers what his friend Kevin told him about Judy – about what a nice girl she is, and how he must always respect her.

And because of David's kindness to her, and also to his many friends and fans, Judy respects David, too. She would respect him for his many good qualities even if he hadn't accomplished what he has as an entertainer.

Now that Kevin is gone, he has left this legacy of mutual respect between David and Judy: a legacy upon which they each have built. He has also left them the gift of their friendship for each other, which has helped to sustain David through these most exciting yet most difficult days of his life, when he needs true friends so much.

David Cassidy was heartbroken when his good friend Kevin died . . . so heartbroken that he even spoke out for publication about the tragedy, hoping that it would serve as a lesson to his many fans about the terrible things that the illegal use of drugs can do to even the finest young people. You may have read what David said on the subject.

But although David is saddened by the great tragedy of Kevin's death, he and Judy will always be grateful that Kevin lived and that they knew him for at least a little while.

And they will always be grateful to Kevin himself for the friendship they share. They only wish that he could be here still to enjoy with them the wonderful life they are living today.

They miss him, they feel infinitely sad about his tragic death – but they cherish the memory of this talented lost, young boy, and they hope he has found peace at last.

*Chapter Eight*

# THE GIRL WHO HURT DAVID ...
## WITHOUT MEANING TO

Although he doesn't know her name, David Cassidy will never forget the girl who hurt him soon after he became a star in 1970. For although she caused him a great deal of distress and inconvenience at the time, she changed his life ... for the better!

She did it by making it necessary for David to move out of his apartment in Laurel Canyon, a woodsy, informal part of Los Angeles which he had come to know as home.

David had loved his sparsely-furnished little pad high up in Laurel Canyon, with its sweeping view of the hills. It was a place he would never forget – the place where it had all begun to happen for him – everything he had studied for, worked for and dreamed of for years. He had moved into it as an unknown young singer and actor. By the time he left it, he had already enjoyed his first exciting taste of stardom.

Yes, David was forced to move out of the funky little apartment he had shared with his roommate, Sam Hyman, and his two dogs – Sam and Sheesh. For suddenly it was no longer really his apartment. It had become public property, with this girl and her friends hurting him without really meaning to.

They did it by robbing David of the privacy he so desperately needed. He could no longer go on working 14-hour days, only to come home and find himself on public display, when all he wanted was the chance to rest and be alone and recharge his batteries for the next day's incessant demands on his energies.

How had it happened? How had these people found out where David lived?

The girl had obtained David's phone number and his address by telephoning all the animal hospitals in town until she located the one where David had taken his dogs for veterinary care.

The pet hospital was told by this persistent young lady that she was one of David's relatives, apparently, and that she needed to get hold of his address and phone number.

Why anyone at the hospital should think that a relative of David's would have to be asking for his address and number is not known. But the girl's excuse must have been a good one, for she was rewarded with this privileged information. And she didn't hesitate to use it.

From then on, David had no privacy whatsoever in his own home. For although he is devoted to his fans, enjoys getting together with them for visits as much as possible, and tries to please them with his performances, he is only human. He needs his few spare moments of rest and seclusion, if he is to carry on his work without collapsing.

Nearly all of David's real fans understand this and respect his privacy. But this particular girl and her friends were just too enthusiastic. The phone calls to David's unlisted number at all hours, the parade of unknown visitors at his front door – all these made David's life at home impossible, and he had to move as quickly as he could – and as *secretly* as possible, lest he be followed to his new residence.

So he got together a group of fellows he knew, loyal friends who, he felt sure, would not reveal his new address, a house in the Hollywood Hills above the Sunset Strip. He asked them if they would help him move. Of course they agreed. And then David rented a U-Drive truck and put his relatively few belongings into it.

There was his prized set of drums – *that* had to be handled with particular care. He had blasted the rafters many times with those drums, with some of his buddies joining him for an impromptu rock session – "'jamming," as David called it.

And there was his guitar, which he had learned to play with effortless professionalism. Nobody was going to be disappointed if *he* was asked to play the guitar in public – he'd decided that long ago.

In fact, he had originally started playing the guitar as a youngster, when he first realized that it would come in handy one day in the career he so much wanted as a singer and actor.

There was a set of amplifiers to send his music out across the surrounding hills – fortunately, the neighborhood had been somewhat short on neighbors. And there was his prized collection of records, including those made by his musical idol, Jimi Hendrix, who had recently died tragically young.

There were other cherished belongings to be moved: books for those fleeting moments he could spare between work and sleep, and his 23-inch color television set, which he used mainly for studying his own work, something he did very critically and with a complete lack of conceit. He found little chance to use the television set otherwise, for there simply wasn't time.

But there was almost no furniture. David didn't like it, at least while he was living in that apartment, and he'd had little more than a bed for sleeping and a milk crate for sitting in his nearly bare room. His roommate, Sam, with a room of his own, had lived in similarly Spartan style.

Sam was an understanding sort, and he had known David for years. So he could sense instinctively when David wanted to be alone – which was fairly often. Sometimes they saw little of each other for days at a time.

As Shirley Jones, with whom David has a good relationship, has said in speaking of her famous stepson: "He's a private person."

David's introspective attitude may well have begun because his parents were away from him so much during his childhood. His dad, Jack Cassidy, and his mother, Evelyn, were often out touring the country either separately or together in stage or night club shows during David's early years. So he was often left in the care of his maternal grandparents, whose house in New Jersey became the only home he knew for much of his childhood.

His parents' divorce when he was six, and his father's subsequent marriage to Shirley Jones, changed his life forever and forced him to become more self-reliant emotionally, now that he didn't see his father as often.

As David told me, he knows that Shirley Jones did not break up his parents' marriage. But he does blame show business.

For he still believes that the marriage might have worked out if his folks had not been in the entertainment field. The traveling, the pressures, the separations caused by work – all these helped break up their marriage.

Yet even though he knew from a very early age how hazardous show business could be in the lives of those who pursued it – and in the lives of those they loved – the business attracted David from his earliest childhood. That was why he looked forward to a career in that field throughout his school years, although most of his friends didn't know it at the time.

And yet, once David was actually in television, the pressures of fame began to build up in his own life. Not only was there all the fan mail to be taken care of, there were already interviewers demanding to know his innermost secrets at their very first meeting.

No longer could he enjoy a casual hot dog or hamburger with a girl friend without creating a stir. He was grateful for the fact that the public was so interested in him, and he enjoyed meeting people who liked him and admired his work. Yet he knew that his privacy was fast disappearing.

And although being recognized in public was flattering and a sign of success, David has always been an intensely shy person, so he found it difficult at first to know what to say in the face of a flood of compliments from strangers, an experience he was not used to.

When I asked David if he ever got uptight about being on public display when this meant being frequently mobbed by crowds of admirers, he answered quite frankly: "Yes, I hide! Whenever I can, I run for cover." And he wasn't kidding. He admitted that such a strong reaction from people had at first made him feel "weird . . . insecure."

Later he learned to adjust to it better. For this he could thank his father, mother and stepmother, show business veterans all.

For Jack, Evelyn, Shirley, and Ruth Aarons knew that David had chosen a career which seemed destined to keep him in the public eye for years to come and they wanted him to be happy and at ease with his fame.

So they spent many hours talking to him, trying to teach him how to face the public, and advising him on his duty as an entertainer to share at least a part of his private life with that public.

David learned quickly. And yet, David did not take naturally to fame and adulation, because of his native shyness. But he soon realized that he had to accept it gracefully.

Nor did he go for flashy Mod clothes, although he learned to wear them with real flair when he had to. He much preferred old jeans, a sweat shirt and a comfortable pair of tennis shoes which rapidly became his trademark.

By the time the first episode of *The Partridge Family* was televised in the fall of 1970, accompanied by the release of Bell Records' first Partridge Family album and single, people were already calling David Cassidy "the next Bobby Sherman."

But these were strange words to David. It was not that he disliked or didn't admire Bobby – the two have always gotten along just fine. But although he had longed for fame in the past, he had thought of it more in terms of the kind of success his father and stepmother enjoyed.

Jack Cassidy was a Tony winner on Broadway for his performance in *She Loves Me*, and his success had inspired David to head immediately for Broadway when he began his own efforts to build a career in show business. Shirley Jones had won the Oscar for her role in *Elmer Gantry*. Although she had begun her career under the auspices of the legendary Broadway songwriters and producers, Rodgers and Hammerstein, she had served an apprenticeship in the theatre which began with her job as a chorus girl in one of their hit shows. And his mother, under the stage name of Evelyn Ward, had replaced Gwen Verdon on Broadway as the star of *New Girl in Town* after working for many years to reach that position.

David, in other words, came from a show-business family with a certain kind of tradition. His people were honored, respected performers who had taken a certain amount of time to reach success. And when they did achieve stardom, they were still able to go anywhere without creating a disturbance of any kind. They were admired by the public, yet they did not arouse screams and adulation among their admirers.

But David belonged to a different generation, and he was a different type of performer, although no less talented than the other members of his family. His fame was relatively sudden, and it was of the most intense kind. His picture was soon on the cover of almost every teenage magazine month after month, and he even appeared on the cover of *Life* magazine as America's top teenage idol.

Like Elvis Presley, David learned to accept and live with this kind of intense public attention. But he also came to realize from experience that if he was to give his fans the kind of performances that deserved their praise, he needed at least a minimum of rest and privacy in his few rare hours at home. He could not be on stage 24 hours a day, or he would collapse.

And that was why, when the location of his Laurel Canyon apartment became widely known, he moved from one hillside to another, taking his few prized possessions with him, and hoping that he would find a bit of rest and privacy again.

Happily for David, in time he came to love his new house, which was much roomier than his old apartment and far better furnished. He found it was a delightful place for giving parties for his friends, or just rapping with a few of them when he had a few moments free from his busy schedule.

Eventually he was glad that he had moved there, for in doing so he had indeed found a new kind of life. And, strangely enough, for that he could thank the unknown girl who had tracked him down so cleverly – the girl who had forced him to leave his old home and his old life behind.

## Chapter Nine

## CAN A TEENAGE IDOL
## LEAD A NORMAL LIFE?

No way! A teenage idol like David Cassidy can *not* lead what most people his age – or anyone else, for that matter – would call a normal life. As we have seen, David learned that fact quickly. But to his credit, he tries to lead as normal an existence as possible. And in many ways he succeeds.

First let's learn a little more about how he got to be a teenage idol in the first place – from David himself.

How did he go from being the still-childish David Cassidy who threw candy at his teacher in junior high school, the troubled teenager who had so many problems during his high-school days, to the self-controlled and very special person who burst upon the national consciousness as the idol of teenage girls all over the country?

"How did you get interested in performing, David?" I asked him not long ago.

"It started when I first saw my father perform on the Broadway stage, when I was three years old," he replied. "You remember I told you how excited I got? Well, ever since that time I can remember singing! And later on, another influence was my stepmom, Shirley Jones."

"Did you study singing when you were a child?" I wondered.

"No, I never took any singing lessons when I was a child. But I did sing with a choir in church for seven years, and I was their soloist. So that helped," he said.

"I know that you studied singing in New York when you were 18. How long did that go on before you won your first Broadway role?"

"It was only three or four months. Meanwhile, I was

auditioning for roles during my lunch breaks while working in a textile mill in the garment district."

David hated working in New York's garment district while he was waiting and hoping and studying for a chance at a good role on Broadway. But he still retains a fondness for New York City itself.

"When I am there, I enjoy it, except in the wintertime," David said. "What I have is recollections of when I was much younger. Although I lived in New Jersey when I was a boy, I was in New York a lot to visit my father, who lived there." This was after his parents' separation.

"New York is a very special place for me," David admitted. "I don't know why. I guess I'm just sentimental or something . . ."

"What kind of role did you play when you finally landed a job on Broadway in *The Fig Leaves Are Falling*?" I wanted to know.

"Well, it was a musical. And I played the son of Barry Nelson and Dorothy Loudon. But the show wasn't a hit! However, the job lasted for several months, counting rehearsals."

"And then what kind of role did you play on your first television show when you came back to California?"

"I had the role of a young thief in one of the *Ironside* episodes. That was my first television part in Hollywood," he recalled. Then he added with a smile, "And I wasn't very good in the part!

"But I learned from it, and after that I did guest shots on a lot of other programs during 1969. I really started to work like crazy at the end! I was fortunate enough to get a couple of really good things, and that kept the roles coming.

"Finally, in December of 1969, I was cast as Keith in the pilot for *The Partridge Family*," he noted.

"That role really changed your life. How long after you tested for it did you find out that you had definitely won the part?" I asked him.

78

"About a week after the test," David replied. But, he noted, that was not the end of waiting to see whether he really had scored his big breakthrough.

First the pilot film had to be approved as the basis for a series by the network. And even when the approval had come through, there were still problems.

"The people at Screen Gems were very confident that the show would be a success even before the good ratings came out," David recalled. "And I myself thought that we had a well-made pilot. And the rest of the episodes pretty much kept up to that standard. But I was afraid we would have a lot of heavy competition from Andy Griffith, whose new series was on opposite our show.

"He's a television superstar, that man!" David said admiringly. "His *Andy Griffith Show* was number one for years. But I felt our show was strong enough that if people would see it once, then they'd watch it again, unless they were really devout Andy Griffith fans."

As it turned out, *The Partridge Family* completely outrated Andy Griffith's comeback series and the Griffith show was quickly canceled. The same thing happened to *The Name of the Game*, which had been a popular show for years. It was canceled, too, when it couldn't compete with *The Partridge Family* in that time slot.

With the weekly television exposure of his hit TV series, which in turn promoted his Bell Records releases into hits – since the show featured a new song each week – it was a natural step for David to go into concerts.

But when it came to concerts – as, indeed, in all his other work – David was not content to ride on his popularity. He was determined from the very beginning to give his fans a show which was entertaining and professional in every respect, to do a goodly number of songs rather than making just a brief appearance, and to see that he was surrounded by the best people both on and off the stage.

His back-up musicians and the other entertainers on the bill are all top-notch performers, and the concerts are

79

organized and promoted by experienced professionals. David's personal managers, Ruth H. Aarons and Jim Flood of the Aarons Management Corporation office – Jim is also David's publicist – are both actively involved in the planning of the concerts.

His busy schedule keeps David working during almost every one of his waking hours. Even his weekends, which used to provide precious moments of relaxation, are now often taken up with trips around the country to appear in concerts. That's why I wondered what he does in those rare moments when he finds himself at home with some spare time.

"Nothing, really!" he grinned as he responded to my question. "I sleep a lot. And I enjoy playing the guitar with friends. You know, there's not that much time for me to do anything during the week. And on those weekends when I'm not working, I just like to relax – maybe go scuba diving, skiing or hiking in the canyons above Malibu."

"You certainly have come a long way from those unhappy days in high school," I noted. "Let's talk about that for a minute, to see what you learned. You've said that you fell under the influence of the wrong crowd of friends at University High. Do you think it's important for young people not to let others influence them too much?"

"Yes. If you just want to be yourself, to just do what you want and be what you are, that's cool. But if you let others influence you the wrong way, as I did, then you're *not* being yourself," David said firmly. "I'm lucky that I managed to change."

"But although your past troubles are over, don't you have to face a whole bunch of new pressures now that you're a popular performer?" I asked.

"Oh, yes – I mean, absolutely!" he agreed. "It just never stops. They merely become different pressures, you know?

"But pressures are like roadblocks," David pointed out. "I just sort of went under them and around them and over

80

them, and I found a way to deal with them. Before that experience in high school and what it taught me, I couldn't deal with them."

"Others who've been in a somewhat similar position to yours have *not* been able to deal with the pressures," I reminded David. "How did you feel when your musical idol, Jimi Hendrix, died of an overdose of drugs?"

He frowned. "When I heard about it, I spent all day trying to forget. That cat was like my idol for so long! If there's one person that I can say I always wanted to meet, it was Jimi Hendrix, ever since the first time I heard him.

"I saw Jimi in concert about six times," David revealed, "and I think he really contributed so much to rock music – was such an influence on it. He had so much as a musician. Wow, could he play the guitar! It's such a pity that he died."

David's pressures, in a way, have been more serious than those that faced Jimi Hendrix. For Hendrix was not mobbed by fans wherever crowds might gather, as David is. That alone would make a "normal" life impossible. If it's a young people's hangout, David has to avoid it or risk being responsible for a riot.

And whereas Jimi was mainly a record and concert star, David has a weekly television series to do as well. His incredibly heavy workload keeps him from having the time to do many of the little things that make up a part of most people's lives.

"How do you feel about acting in a television series?" I asked David.

"The creativity is pretty limited," he admitted, "because this medium is all cut and dried. But I learned an incredible amount about filming from working on television!

"I learned technique," he explained. "That's not all of what acting is about, but it's a good part of it. A lot has to do with an attitude – with having confidence in yourself."

It took David a whole show to gain that confidence, for when he made his TV debut on *Ironside* he didn't have it.

"The lack of confidence was there – I could see it," David confesses. "I don't think very many other people saw it, but some did! A camera shows up a lot of things, and you see a lot of things when you watch yourself on TV."

"Although you feel that working on a television series is not creative, do you feel happy that you're on *The Partridge Family*?" I asked him.

"Yes, I'm happy. We've had good scripts, I think. You're always going to get certain scripts that are better than others, but the shows have been good shows.

"For me personally, it's steady work, and there are good people involved in the show. But I'm a bit frustrated, I must confess. I would like to be doing other things, too. I'd like to be able to devote even more time to singing. I just wish I had more time to do both – acting and singing!"

"Speaking of your acting and singing – although you're over 21 years old, you still sound like a teenager on *The Partridge Family*," I noted. "Your voice isn't still changing, is it?"

He laughed. "No. It sounds like it, but it's not! I think my voice is just like that. It's been raspy. I don't know why, but it's that way. Sometimes it's not, though."

"Do you smoke?" I asked. "Maybe that's why your voice is raspy."

He shook his head. "I used to smoke when I was a teenager, I'll admit. But I don't smoke anymore."

Somehow smoking led us to drinking – to talking about drinking, I mean! – and I asked David, "How did you celebrate your 21st birthday? Did you drink?"

"I went out to a restaurant with my roommate, Sam Hyman, and some other friends, and I had my favorite dish, which is steamed clams. I go crazy for them! So I ordered buckets of steamed clams.

"I don't like to drink that much, but I did that night," he admitted, "because my friends wanted to see me do it. After I ordered my drink, I said, 'Don't you want to see my I.D?'

"The waitress thought for a minute and then said, 'Okay – sure!' I pulled the identification out and showed it to her, and it was ridiculous. But – we had a really good time!'"

Unfortunately, such good times are increasingly rare for David, as far as visiting public places is concerned. He must avoid many of the places he likes for fear of creating a disturbance by his very presence. He can't enjoy himself in public the way he used to, because of his effect on people.

Sometimes it gets downright embarrassing. For example, one day David was at Marineland, a popular Southern California tourist attraction, filming an episode of *The Partridge Family* about ecology, a subject which concerns him deeply.

But it was hard to concentrate on his work with screaming crowds watching his every move between takes. And at one point so many teenage girls converged on him at once that he was afraid that either they or he – or possibly both – would get hurt. So David ran into a nearby men's room to escape them.

It didn't work. The girls followed him right in, which must have been a startling event for any other males who were in the room at that moment!

And then there's the matter of privacy at his home. After he was forced to move from Laurel Canyon to the Hollywood Hills because a girl had obtained his address and given it out to her friends, David took great precautions to keep his new address from becoming widely known.

David rented the house completely furnished from its owner, a popular Hollywood restaurateur. It had a swimming pool and a yard for his dogs to run around in.

The house itself was filled with beautiful paintings and other art objects, yet the furniture and the rugs were informal and colorful in an unpretentious way.

"I could never live in a house where I couldn't put my feet up anyplace I wanted to," David says. That's why he enjoyed living in his Hollywood Hills home, which he considered "warm . . . tasteful . . . modern but rustic."

Although various efforts were made to keep unwanted intruders from learning David's new address, that didn't prevent a burglar from looting the place of some of David's possessions soon after he moved in. But perhaps the thief who took David's color television set and some of his clothes hadn't known that David lived there.

Eventually, though, more and more people did learn where David lived, despite all his attempts at secrecy. People could just open his unlocked gate and walk up to the door and knock, at any hour of the day or night. Finally David realized that he would have to move once more.

Now David lives in the San Fernando Valley. If too many people find out where he lives this time, at least they won't be able to get inside – hopefully.

And yet behind the locked gates a very real human being, one who has much the same joys and sorrows as the very fans who idolize him. David Cassidy is devoted to his family and to his old friends.

He told me that the two keepsakes he cherishes most are "a medallion that my mother gave me to wear around my neck, and a ring that my father gave me."

And then he added, "The ring came off my finger when a girl came up to the foot of the stage and took hold of my hand when I was shaking hands with fans during a personal appearance. I really felt terrible when I realized that it was gone, because it represented one of my ties with my family.

"But the girl gave it back to me after the show. Wasn't that nice of her? From now on, though, I won't take the ring with me when I make a personal appearance – or at least," he added with a laugh, "if I'm wearing it, I won't hold anyone's hand!'"

David loves his fame despite its occasional disadvantages. He knows how many talented actors and singers are out of work, and he feels that he's a very lucky person.

Above all, he is truly grateful to the devoted fans who made his success possible, even though a few inconsiderate individuals have been responsible for invading his privacy to such an extent that he has been forced twice to move out of his own home.

Yet the people who seem to mean the most to David, outside of his family, are the friends he has known since his schooldays. For it is they who help him to lead as nearly normal a life as it is possible for him to have under the circumstances.

"They're kind of like mirrors," David told me. "They let me see myself as I really am. In the business I'm in, I would lose my perspective without them, because they're really good, honest friends.

"They're 'down home' – they're really my kind of people!" he exclaimed enthusiastically. "They don't try to be something they're not. They're always themselves, so I'm myself around them, and I feel comfortable and secure when I'm with them.

"I can't specifically say what each friend means to me," David admitted. "But I don't think I would be able to do what I'm doing, in this situation I've been thrown into, if it weren't for them. And I'm able to share a lot with them.

"I'm most fortunate to have nice friends that I really like," David said gratefully. "It's out of sight!"

## Chapter Ten

# DAVID RAPS ABOUT GIRLS

"I don't get a chance to meet too many girls," David Cassidy admitted to me recently, "because there isn't much of an opportunity."

How can someone who frequently gives two concerts a weekend before thousands of admiring teenage girls say something like that? How could David find it difficult to meet girls?

Because it happens to be true. David is whisked to the location of each concert under guard, does his concert, greets and shakes hands with as many girls as he safely can during and after the concert, then quickly has to leave the concert location and the city to go on to another concert or back to Hollywood.

And when he's in Hollywood, his working hours are so long that he seldom has so much as an hour to himself on weekdays, he told me. On weekends he either has to fly off for concerts – or he's so exhausted that he has to use most of the weekend to rest or get away somewhere by himself to clear his head of the exhausting pressures of the week.

And unfortunately, when he does get a chance to meet a fan in a situation where there's a moment or two to talk and get to know each other, too often the poor girl is so shaken by the opportunity of meeting her idol at last that conversation becomes next to impossible for her, and the meeting becomes one of signing autographs and, on David's part, trying to assure his admirer that he's only human like anyone else. It's hardly the kind of a situation that might lead to two young people getting to know about each other and, perhaps, becoming involved romantically.

That's why the list of David Cassidy's dates is a rather small one, and why he has no "best girl" at all.

David has said that many actresses are "just too preoccupied with themselves." And yet, because his work puts him into contact with actresses so much, several of his dates have been actresses.

So the actresses he has dated must have something special in David's mind, despite what he has said about actresses being too self-centred ... something that has kept them from falling into the traps of egotism and selfishness that ruin too many actresses' personalities.

Three of the actresses David has dated, and possibly more, share certain traits which David has long found attractive in females. So let's see what those three girls have that other actresses, by and large, may not – what it is that attracts David enough to make him ask for a date and then become good friends with the girl. What qualities in girls appeal to David?

To this writer, the ideal seems to resemble in some ways the woman whom David likes and respects more than any other woman in the world, with the single exception of his mother. The woman he so admires is Shirley Jones, his stepmother for 15 years and the top star of *The Partridge Family*.

And yet Shirley, by being such a thoroughly admirable woman, has set such a high standard of womanhood before David's eyes that it may well be difficult for any of the girls he meets to live up to it.

It has even been suggested that until he finds a girl who meets that standard fully, David Cassidy will take his time about getting married.

Indeed, one of the people who has made that suggestion, or at least has agreed with it when it was put to him, is David himself.

In his more pensive moments, David has admitted to me in explaining why he doesn't want to get married yet, that he is waiting to find a wife with Shirley's wonderful qualities.

He lists other reasons, too, all of them perfectly valid. Yet David *would* like to find a wife who is like Shirley Jones.

So let's take a closer look at one girl he knows, Susan Dey, in order to find out David's reaction to her.

Susan Dey was only 17 years old when she began work on *The Partridge Family*, but had already gained a great deal of poise by doing television commercials for a brand of candy bars, hair dryers and other products.

Yet she was well aware of her almost complete lack of dramatic training when she began work as a regular member of *The Partridge Family*, and was grateful to David when he did his best to put her at ease by befriending her and assuring her that all would be well.

Indeed, although they do not actually date each other, David *has* taken Susan out to eat occasionally, since she is such a good friend.

But he told me, "We don't go to many places together. I don't see her that much. I see her every day when *The Partridge Family* is filming, because we work together, so there isn't so much of a need to see each other outside.

"But I take Susan to lunch sometimes. We talk about the show, or about the East Coast, since we both come from the East originally," David noted. Since they both began their careers in New York at about the same time, they have many memories of that city to talk about, even though they never met while they were working there. But their friendship has never turned into any kind of a romance.

Right now, David doesn't date *any* girl very often. "I'm just working to get to the point where I won't be too busy – because it won't always be like this," he realizes. He's been told many times, and has seen in the cases of other performers, that the popularity of teenage idols does not continue on an intensely high level for more than a few years. He's well aware of that, and it doesn't seem to bother him.

In fact, he says, "Maybe in a couple of years I will be able to do what I want to do. But right now I just have to concentrate on working." High on the list of things David wants to do is finding some time for a real romance.

But even now, David manages to steal some spare moments in which he can relax and enjoy himself. "I like to go out hiking in the canyons near Los Angeles sometimes," he told me. "There are a lot of groovy canyons, like Tuna Canyon and others. Or I'll drive by the beach, up to Point Dume, north of L.A.; I like to go there and just take my guitar, and sit and think.

"But I don't go by myself all the time! Sometimes I go with a friend of mine, sometimes with a girl.

"I like to be near the water, because I like to scuba dive," David explained. "But the main thing about getting away is that when you're in the city there is so much pressure. It's like, really, a hassle! I'm more comfortable when I'm out in the country."

Although marriage plays no part in David's immediate plans, and despite the fact that many of his trips to the beach or the canyons are made alone, it would be inaccurate to say that David actually *avoids* romance.

"I've thought a lot about getting involved," he admits. And then – surprisingly, considering his fantastic popularity – he adds: "There have been girls that I wanted to take out that wouldn't go out with me for one reason or the other.

"Maybe they were hung up – or were involved already with someone else," he speculates. "But if I get no reaction from a girl, I don't pursue her!

"I don't remember *ever* having done that, because I'm not that type of person," says David, who has always been sensitive to rejection. "If I get turned off by a girl, I stay turned off." He knows better than to court heartbreak and embarrassment by making a fool of himself over a girl who couldn't care less.

"Everybody isn't available for you. It's important to realize that," David believes, on the basis of his own personal experience. And he adds, in an understatement considering his very specialized situation, "It's hard to find someone who wants and needs the same things *you* do."

What does David look for in a relationship with a girl?

When I put that question to him, he thought for a moment, and then replied slowly, "Trust and honesty between two people is important. You have to have that – and love!"

Remembering that David had been a somewhat lonely boy at times during his teenage years despite his many friends – and that he had never really had a steady girl friend when I had first known him – I thought of the contrast between that boy and this young man, pursued now by adoring girls wherever he goes.

"When girls come on strong for you," I asked him, "do you ever wonder, 'Where were you when I needed you?' Does that thought ever occur to you?"

He shook his head. "No, because that doesn't really turn me on. Somebody coming on strong doesn't turn me on." Apparently David finds it most appealing when a girl neither "comes on strong" nor rejects him outright. He likes to be the pursuer – but only when the girl wants to be pursued!

In fact, he doesn't want to be pursued by *any* girl too strongly, either in his private or his public life, since he wants to be the one who's doing the chasing. I learned this when I asked him, "What about your relationship with your fans? You work almost every waking hour trying to turn out work that will please them. I know you've performed many individual acts of kindness for your fans.

"And yet you still have a lot of shyness in you, as you did when I first knew you. You've said that *groups* of people really psych you out when they start rushing at you suddenly, and that you rush the other way. Is that still true?"

He nodded, a sheepish grin on his face. "I *always* run away. It's like I've *got* to run! I don't know what to do!"

"That's probably what they like about you – that you're obviously shy," I noted.

David shrugged helplessly. "I just run!"

"You're like the average guy who finds himself in this

position," I suggested.

"Yeah – I am! I am no different than anyone else," David pointed out. "I don't pretend to be. I like the things everybody likes, and yet I'm an individual, as individual as anyone can *be* in this kind of society. It is hard for me to meet people, because I don't go out that much." And then he added, as if I didn't already know: "It is *hard* to go out."

"I guess people rush up to you wherever you go in public," I told him.

"Well, not everywhere. I can go places. It's just people in general. I find that I can't do anything inconspicuously anymore. Everything I do everybody knows about! Everybody sees me.

"So I have to be cool. I have to be careful, because it is uncomfortable to go out to a restaurant on a date now, or even when I'm alone.

"It's hard to cope when people are hitting me for my autograph and telling me how much they like my work. It's really nice of them, and I really appreciate it. But there is a time when I don't want to hear that, when I want to rap like I'm rapping with you now. So consequently I'm home more than anyplace else during my free time. I can do anything in my house. I do what I want when I'm home. It's like my hideaway!"

"Do you want to get married in the near future, or would you like to stay single for a long time?" I asked him.

"I'd like to stay single until I'm 25, maybe, or maybe a little older. Before I get married, there are a lot of things that I have to do, that I want to do," he replied. "And I really don't have the time to devote to someone now.

"There are so *many* things I want to do!" he exclaimed. "I want to travel and see the world. . . ." And indeed, not long after we talked, David did take off on a trip to Europe during a *matus* in the production schedule for *The Partridge Family*.

"I can't take on the responsibility of marriage yet," he continued. "I have too much of a problem with *myself* right

92

now. I'm having trouble just coping with *me*, let alone someone else – supporting someone else, taking care of someone else.

"So the chances are, I won't marry in the near future. And yet – you never know!" he added with a sudden smile. "I could meet someone tomorrow and say, 'This is it!'"

Then he paused and added soberly, "But that would be unfortunate, I would say ... both for her and for me. Because I'm not ready for it now."

David had stressed repeatedly, as we discussed the various girls in his life, that he was not involved in a serious romance with any of them. So I asked him now, "Are you afraid, perhaps, that if you were deeply involved with one girl right now, that might make some other girls resent her?"

He shook his head. "I think if I really loved someone, it wouldn't matter."

"Knowing you, I don't think it would," I agreed.

And, as if to emphasize the point, he repeated: "I don't think it would really matter. I don't think about that."

"I don't believe you would censor your emotions," I told him knowing his extreme sincerity and honesty in such matters.

"I wouldn't. I wouldn't be able to!" he exclaimed.

And perhaps that is why David feels that if he met the right girl he would get married, even if he felt that the time was not really right for it.

During our conversation, David revealed, in a way, the kind of girl he wants his future wife to be.

He had just expressed regret that Shirley Jones had not been nominated for an Emmy Award for her performance on *The Partridge Family*. But then he had added quickly that being a wife and mother was really much more important to Shirley herself.

At this point I told him, "I think Shirley is the kind of woman that you're really waiting to meet before you get married."

And David admitted instantly, in that very honest way he has with *all* his friends, "Oh, yeah. . . ." And then he repeated wistfully: "Oh, yeah. She's just a nice human being."

There is one sad note to add to this story. In January, 1972, some months after I talked to David about Shirley, she and David's father, Jack Cassidy, announced a trial separation.

How ironic that the two women David most admires, his mother and his stepmother, eventually found themselves unable to stay happily married to his father, a proud and talented man who, as David told me, has sometimes found it difficult to be in a situation where his wife and son attained success far more quickly than he, and a tremendous kind of success at that.

Perhaps these pressures contributed to the trial separation of Jack Cassidy and Shirley Jones. Many other factors undoubtedly entered into the situation, in any case.

But whether or not the marriage of Jack and Shirley is eventually saved, that will not affect David's admiration for Shirley or his closeness to her, as they continue to co-star in *The Partridge Family* and to maintain their valued friendship.

Yet with this latest example of family marital problems to sadden him and make him cautious, it will be no surprise if David Cassidy waits a long, long time before venturing on a marriage of his own.

## Chapter Eleven

## "MY MOTHER SACRIFICED
EVERYTHING FOR ME"

Although David Cassidy likes and admires his television
mother, Shirley Jones, so much that he hopes his future wife
will have Shirley's best qualities, he is even more devoted to
his real mother, the former Evelyn Ward.

And, because he is such a devoted son, it worries him
when he sees that his own mother is largely overlooked by
people who write about his close relationship to Shirley.

I had known this, but had not realized the extent to which
David is concerned about the matter until one day when we
were discussing the two women in a conversation at his
home.

"Do you know what I'd like?" he asked me suddenly.
"I'd like you to write something about my mother and all
that she has given up for my sake. You know, my mother
sacrificed everything for me – everything!

"And she's kind of gone unmentioned, because she's not
in the limelight the way Shirley is or the way my father is. In
a way, she's been pushed aside when people have written
about me.

"That bothers me, because I'm about the only thing she
has," David said, with obvious concern in his voice. "The
only thing she has in the world.

"Yet she's not getting the proper credit for what she has
done for me, because it's better publicity, I guess, to write
about Shirley, since she and I are both in *The Partridge
Family* and she plays my mother on the show.

"I feel that my mother is really responsible for any success I have today," David confessed, "more so than any-

body else. She molded me, you know. She was the biggest influence on my life, and I guess she's proud of me. So I think it would do her good to – to sort of get a pat on the back, because she certainly deserves it!

"She has made *so* many sacrifices for me," David pointed out. "In fact, she sacrificed her own career for me. She was starring on Broadway, and she gave it up, because her whole thing was to be a mother – just to be a mother. You know, after she and my dad were divorced when I was six, she didn't remarry for about five years. She devoted all her time to *me*." During those five crucial years of David's life, when he particularly felt the heartbreak and loss of his parents' divorce – which had been preceded, in fact, by a long separation – David had the constant comfort of his mother's reassuring presence and love to make things easier for him.

He told me that he first became conscious of his mother's sacrifices for him when he was 10 years old.

"That's when we moved out here to California from New Jersey," he recalled. "We lived in a small town there, and she wanted me to have something more, because there are a lot of closed minds in small towns, and she wanted me to see more of the world.

"We were living in West Orange with my grandmother and my grandfather," David explained. "They were good people. But I wasn't experiencing enough.

"There are so many things you lose, spending your life in a small town like that. I go back there now and visit, and the people there are really nice. But it's such a small world!

"My mother didn't want that town to become my *whole* world," David emphasized. "She wanted to open my eyes to what else there was in life."

Suddenly his voice grew sad, with perhaps a tinge of guilt in it. "You might say that in opening up my world, she closed down her own world," he told me, "because right then she had found quite a lot of success on Broadway for the very first time, replacing Gwen Verdon as the star of *New Girl in Town.*

David and friends getting ready for a big number

David af home

"And just when she was in demand in New York, she left for my sake. But once you leave the place where your career is going well, it's hard to get started again somewhere else," David noted.

"My mother didn't really have too much money," he revealed, "and it was very hard for us to get by in Los Angeles. We found a house, but she couldn't get a job for a while.

"It was a completely different place! When you're working in New York, if you come out here you don't know anybody. And the doors are very hard to knock down, you know?"

He paused, remembering. "The same thing happened to me when I started in show business. But I was a little more fortunate. Because when I started working, I *kept* working, and I didn't stop. But my mother started working, and then she gave the whole thing up for me."

He smiled. "Of course, she said that she wanted it that way. But I think it was simply more important to her that she give me what she felt I needed." And then the smile was gone as he added, "And I *did* need it. . . .

"She did find some work out here eventually," David recalled, "but when I was 11 years old she gave it up and married Elliot Silverstein."

Silverstein was then a popular television director. But he was ambitious to get into movie production, and a few years after the marriage he won a job directing *Cat Balou*, starring Jane Fonda and Lee Marvin. The picture won Marvin an Academy Award and was the beginning of Silverstein's success as a movie director.

"My mother still wanted to work," David pointed out. "She wanted a career. But her marriage and my welfare were more important to her. So she gave up her career.

"It was largely for me that she stopped working again," David believes. "She was worried that she wouldn't be around when I needed her, and that bothered her. So she gave it up."

He looked at me questioningly to see whether I realized what giving up her career had meant to his mother. As if to emphasize his point, he added, "I know that was really hard on her. And now that I'm on my own, it's hard for her to find work again.

"You see, when you stay out of the business for several years as my mother did, it's difficult to get involved again. She would like to, I think. But *I* wouldn't like her to, not really. . . .

"I think it's a crummy business for her, and I don't want her to be hurt," he said, the concern in his voice very evident. "If you are not 'hot,' per se, you have to take a lot of rejection. There are a lot of unnecessarily cruel people in this business. I know, for I've come up against them myself!

"In fact," David revealed, "my mother was the one who warned me against them when I wanted to get into show business while I was in school. That was why she wanted me to wait until I graduated – why she *insisted* on it.

"She used to say, 'Wait until you're older, and you'll see that there are a lot of bad people in the business!' So I knew that I'd face a lot of rejection.

"I'm glad now that I wasn't allowed to try acting until I graduated from high school," David admitted. "I think about those kids on our show – being around the set all day, surrounded by adults. *That's* no fun! You miss a lot of your childhood that way. Who wants to cope with the problems of show business when you're a child? I have a hard time coping with it all *now*. But when I was younger I *never* could have dealt with it.

"Yet I wanted to run and try it. But my mother said, 'Listen . . . you've got a lot of years ahead, you know. There's plenty of time.'

"She wanted me to grow up, and she insisted that I wait," David noted. And then he added gratefully, "I can never repay her for that, because I don't know where I'd be otherwise. I just *know* I wouldn't be here now, because I couldn't have coped with the business when I was younger."

But although his mother wouldn't let David try show business as a full-time profession while he was still in school, she wisely helped him to prepare for the career that she knew he wanted to have someday.

"When I was about nine or so, she sent me to an acting school back in New Jersey," David continued. "And she always encouraged me to sing, both at home and, as you know, in our church choir." He smiled, remembering. "We even used to sing together at home, my mother and I, a long time ago . . . when I was very young.

"I'll always be grateful that she let me sing in the chorus of one of her shows that time when I was nine, when she was doing summer stock. I couldn't *believe* it, you know? It was the greatest thing! I was so proud to be doing something with the rest of the cast, and to be a part of it all. And in that way she was letting me see what it was all about. . . ."

Now he was very serious again, as he leaned forward to make a point. "A lot of people think I got into show business because of my father, and being around him. And I told you myself that I've been singing ever since I saw him in *Wish You Were Here* on Broadway when I was three years old, which is true. But I wasn't really around my father all that much, because, after all, he and my mother were divorced when I was six years old, and he had to travel a lot because of his career when I was small.

"No, the reason I got some kind of insight into show business was because of my mother . . . because of what I saw through *her*, and what she opened me up to. She made me aware of a lot of things. And by the time I went into show business myself, I was very glad that she had enlightened me about it."

Through his mother, David explained, he was able to develop a philosophy that helped to keep him from being hurt as much as he would otherwise have been by the many rejections that any young performer encounters while trying to get ahead in show business.

"You're bound to take these rejections personally if you're not prepared for them," David told me, "because it's *you* who are being rejected.

"But if you can just think of it as a job, with a piece of merchandise that you have to sell rather than yourself, it helps a lot.

"I'd go in to an audition thinking, 'I'm David Cassidy, and I'm here to sell you something I have – a piece of merchandise. So I'll do a reading and see if you like the merchandise and want to buy it.'

"That helped me a number of times – because I'm so insecure anyway," he confessed. "I think *all* actors are when they walk into that room!

"It's like you are really on the block to be judged, and you have to expect to get your head chopped off a couple of times. It happened to me, *more* than a couple of times, but at last I began to get work.

"My mother helped me to look at the business in that way, and it gave me a positive attitude. I really believe the reason I'm successful is because I had this attitude, and I owe it all to her – totally!

"She was just so *positive* about me. She would say, 'That's going to happen for you because you're *thinking* that way, and because you really want it to happen.' "

He smiled wryly as he admitted. "I was skeptical at first. I'd go, 'Yeah, yeah!' unbelievingly. But I eventually began to adopt my mother's attitude about me.

"When I'd walk into a room to read for a part, I would look around at the other people who were waiting there with me. And I would think, 'I know I should get this part. I'm sure a lot of the other people here are good, but I know I should get this part!'

"And it *worked*," he exclaimed, as if still amazed that it really had. "Every time I did that, it would work! It was a fantastic experience for me – because it made me feel that I could control my own destiny."

"Do you think this philosophy of yours would help
100

others in the same situation?" I asked David.

He nodded. "I definitely think it will work for other people, too. I don't see how it can miss! I just take it from my own experience.

"But if you don't really believe it," he warned, "then it *doesn't* work. I really believed it – I felt positive about it. And I owe that to my mother."

In addition to helping David learn about show business and giving him a positive attitude, it was David's mother who helped him obtain his all-important audition with the Los Angeles Theatre Company between his junior and senior years in high school.

For she realized that the time was only a year away when he would be going out on his own in search of a career. And she felt that working with the theatre group would help him round out his theatrical education, which up to that point had been brief at best.

His work with the Los Angeles Theatre Company was important to David not only from an educational point of view. It provided a crucial uplift for his morale just when that was most vital. It revived David's sagging spirits after the problems of his first two years in high school. For it enabled him to feel that at long last he was doing something concrete in terms of helping his future career, at a time when he was terribly anxious to get started.

A year later, David graduated from Rexford High and, with his mother's blessings and her warm encouragement, he left for New York City to try to crash Broadway.

"When it came time to leave, my mother just let me spread my wings and fly," he recalls gratefully.

And then he brought up a sensitive point as he assured me, "It was fine with her that I was going to stay with my father and Shirley, who were living in a big house at Irvington-on-the-Hudson while they appeared together on Broadway in a musical comedy, *Maggie Flynn*.

"Actually I lived in a little guest house on the estate and

101

spent a lot of time in New York City, so I didn't see too much of them in any case," he noted.

When David won his first Broadway break, his role in the short-lived musical comedy, *The Fig Leaves Are Falling*, he couldn't wait to tell his mother about it.

"She was in California, and I called her immediately," he remembers. "I was ecstatic. I couldn't even talk! I said, 'Ahhhhh . . . guess what? I got a Broadway show!'

"And she said, 'Oh, no! That's fantastic! I *knew* it would happen for you. Now you know it's not that hard to crack the nut.'"

That was the real beginning of David's rapid rise to success, and he was proud and happy that he could share it right away with the one who had prepared him for it – his mother. Each further step along the way was also something for them to share and savor together.

To David Cassidy, his success means a justification of his mother's sacrifices for him. And he admits, without braggadocio and yet with no false modesty, "I think I've done it, you know? Whether I become this big or that big, I don't really think it matters that much.

"The fact is that I feel successful *within myself*. I know that I'm a success – that I've kind of made my own mark. I've *contributed* something, you know? And that's a good feeling. It's satisfying for me."

It's a source of great satisfaction to his mother as well. "She was really pleased about the success of the records and the concerts that I've been doing. She read the reviews of the concerts and was happy for me. And she likes *The Partridge Family*. She thinks it's a good show, and she hopes it runs a long time – and so do I!

"My mother has never minded my working on *The Partridge Family* with Shirley," he noted gratefully. "She has always told me, 'Make up your own mind about people.'

"No, she never put bad thoughts into my mind about my father or Shirley. And I really respect her for that. She never made me think negatively about either of them . . . which is so important . . . *really* important!

"Thanks to my mother and the wise way in which she handled the situation, I was able to accept my father and Shirley much more easily," David noted, "because she never built up a hatred for them in my mind, the way so many mothers do after a divorce, when the father remarries.

"Too many mothers feel hate inside themselves," David observed. "And they try to make their *children* hate, too. But my mother isn't that way – and she never was. For that I'm very grateful."

At the time we talked, David's mother was in the East, and he was looking forward eagerly to their reunion in California. "She already has a place here. She has made arrangements," he told. "She has been with my grandfather back in New Jersey, making sure that he's taken care of before she comes back here." David's grandmother had passed away, so David's mother was particularly concerned about her father's welfare.

David is very devoted to his grandfather, especially because his grandparents played such an important part in raising him when his parents were away touring. And he particularly cherishes the memory of a family reunion that took place on an important date in his life, at his grandfather's house.

"I went back to visit them the day before my 21st birthday. It was Easter, 1971, and I saw my grandfather, my mother, and my cousins and aunts and uncles. They had a small birthday party for me, which was really nice.

"Those are the little pleasures that mean so much in your life," David said quietly. "I feel kind of alone out here, because I'm not really a part of my family or my relatives – I rarely get to see them. So it was nice to go back and say hello to mom."

Yes, it was nice to go back to say hello. But somehow that wasn't enough for David Cassidy.

He wanted to tell his mother something else. He wanted

to say, "Thank you with all my heart ... for giving up so much for me. I owe everything to you!"

That was why he especially wanted this tribute to his mother to be written – so that he could thank her in front of the world.

Because David Cassidy wants the whole world to know that its is his mother who is responsible for his success ... not only for his career success, which is important, but also for the inner satisfaction that money cannot buy.

David loves his father, Jack Cassidy. And Shirley Jones is a good friend he has always respected and liked as a stepmother. But he wants you to know that Shirley is not his mother, except on *The Partridge Family.*

His real mother is alive and well, thank you. Her professional name is Evelyn Ward. You would know that name much better if she had not chosen to dim its lustre in order to let David's star shine more brightly.

David hopes that she will still have her own chance to shine, if that is what she wants. She has brought him up well, taught him what he needs to know, and sent him on his way willingly when it came time for him to spread his own wings.

Now David wants his mother to find some happiness of her own, having given up so much of her happiness for his sake. Success, he feels, she does not really need, for she has already found it in a role that many actresses *never* fill successfully: the role of a mother. But if she still wants a career, that is what David wants for her, too.

Above all, he is glad that she has now returned to California and is living near him once again. For he'd been missing her, and feeling just a bit lonely. He had his father's company, and Shirley's ... but there's no substitute for your own mother, and David thinks he has the best one in the whole world.

He wants *you* to know about her, too. Remember the name – Evelyn Ward. Or, as she was known in her finest performance ... Mom.

## Chapter Twelve

## LOST IN THE DARKNESS

It was midnight, and very dark on the cliffs of Point Dume, which just westward into the Pacific Ocean some 25 miles north of Los Angeles. David Cassidy was walking, stumbling, falling to his knees and painfully getting up again to continue his search for a way back to safety. He was completely lost. Far below, he could hear the ocean crashing among the rocks, and he was afraid.

Worse yet, he didn't have only his own safety to worry about. For at his side, quietly praying to hold back her panic, was his close friend, Judy Strangis.

It was his fault that she was there, risking her life with him – he knew that. For it had been David's idea that they come out here in the first place, along with his roommate, Sam Hyman, and his other buddy, Steve Ross, whom he had known since his schooldays as he had the others. Steve was a talented guitar player, and David had been delighted to use him as an accompanist during his concert appearances around the country.

Now Sam and Steve were also out here on the cliffs somewhere, but David and Judy had become separated from them. He only hoped that his two friends were safe, wherever they were.

It had all started earlier that evening, when David and Sam had made plans to prepare a simple Sunday supper of hot dogs. Just then David had gotten into a phone conversation with Judy, and during their talk he had mentioned that he and Sam were about to make hot dogs.

"Don't cook hot dogs!" Judy had exclaimed sympathetically. "That's ridiculous. My mother has just made spaghetti, and I could bring you some."

105

David didn't want to put Judy to all that bother. But, on the other hand, hot dogs didn't seem like much of a supper, so he gratefully agreed to her idea.

"Okay – I'll get something together," Judy promised.

Her cousin, Spike Jones Jr., the son of the late bandleader, happened to be at her house, and he told Judy, "I'll drive you up there."

So they got together a bunch of delicious Italian food that Judy's mother had made – not only a heaping platter of freshly-cooked spaghetti, but some equally delicious meat balls and a plate of chicken.

When David and Sam greeted Judy at the door, they were surprised and delighted to see all the wonderful food that she had brought them. Judy went into the kitchen and made a delicious salad to go with the feast.

When they all sat down to eat, David and Sam were lavish in their praise of the meal Judy had gotten together for them. As bachelors, neither of whom had very extensive experience in cooking, they were grateful for a break in their usual diet of hot dogs, omelets and other simple fare.

After the meal was over, David had an idea. Why not go to the beach? It was a beautiful, clear night, although the weather was on the chilly side. One of his favorite forms of relaxation was to go to the mountains or the beach for a hike, and this was one of the rare occasions when he had time to do it.

Judy was hesitant, however. "Well . . . I'm working next week, David," she said. "I really shouldn't take a chance on catching cold."

Suddenly Sam volunteered, "I've got a pair of jeans that will fit you!"

And David added, "And I've got a really warm jacket that you can use, Judy."

She smiled, shrugged, and then good-naturedly agreed to go along on the spur-of-the-moment excursion.

Spike had already gone home, after David had promised to see Judy back to her house safely. But his place was soon taken by Steve Ross, whom they picked up on the way.

Once out of the city and driving up the winding Pacific Coast Highway, David felt exhilarated and free. The exhausting pressures and cares of the past week, with its morning-to-night work schedule, seemed to fall away from his shoulders like an unwelcome burden, and he was relaxed and happy.

Ahead of them, the lights of Topanga Beach and Malibu twinkled like a necklace of sparkling jewels. To their left, they could hear the crashing surf of the dark Pacific from time to time. As the car negotiated the many curves on the highway, David felt in full control of the situation and wished that he could go on driving for hours.

And so he passed Malibu and continued on up the coast for several miles, until they had reached Point Dume, the site of an exclusive community of fenced-in homes and almost isolated beaches.

They turned left off the highway, and were soon driving through the darkness along the roads of Point Dume. When they had reached some grass-covered cliffs that led to even higher ground, they parked the car and got out.

"Let's go climbing!" one of the boys said, and the others readily agreed. Sam and Steve had been here before, but this particular area was new to David, and he was anxious to explore it. And Sam and Steve were eager to show it to him.

Higher and higher they climbed, until they reached the top. David and Judy found themselves alone on the high cliffs. Before them spread a beautiful panorama of sea and shore, with the lights of Santa Monica 20 miles to the south of them gleaming mistily in the distance. They themselves were walking now in a gardenlike setting, but they could only discern its outlines in the darkness.

Suddenly Judy exclaimed: "Gosh, I'm exhausted!"

David said, "Okay . . . let's stop here for a second."

He put his arm around Judy protectively and held her close, and for a moment there seemed to be just the two of them left in the world. The only sound came from the crashing surf far below. Hollywood, the studio, the crowds of the city were all very far away now ... so far that it was hard to believe that they existed at all.

They had been climbing and then walking for an hour in the chilly night, and David finally began to feel very cold, for he was wearing only some lightweight jeans, a shirt and a suede jacket.

They began to look around for Sam and Steve, who had promised to be back in five minutes. But five, ten, fifteen minutes went by, and the two boys hadn't come back.

David and Judy didn't want to leave the spot where they had been standing, for then the others wouldn't know where to find them. However, eventually it got so cold that they started to climb down.

As they made their way among the grass and boulders, they kept shouting, "Sam! Steve!" But nobody answered. Only the pounding surf could be heard.

"I can't *see* anything!" Judy said, beginning to sound a little frightened as she stumbled along.

David tried to reassure her. "Well, I think I know the way back to the car. Let's go back there and stay."

"Fine," Judy said uncertainly.

As it turned out, David did *not* know his way back to the car without any flashlight or other illumination to guide him, since he had never been in the area before. And he soon realized that he and Judy were completely lost. But he was determined not to let her see that he, too, was beginning to get worried.

Judy clutched a small handkerchief and began to pray as they made their way downward, narrowly avoiding the cliff's edge at one side of their path.

"Don't worry, Judy – we'll be okay," David told her as reassuringly as possible. And then, as if to convince himself, he repeated: "We'll be okay...." But Judy knew him well, and could detect that he was getting very nervous, even though he tried to sound brave.

108

Sometimes they stumbled into ditches and had to pull themselves out. At other times they would run into unseen boulders, which bruised them badly.

There was no moon now, and it was almost pitch dark. They had to literally feel their way along the clifftop, as the ground in front of them gradually descended – with that sheer drop on one side of them a constant reminder of their danger.

Suddenly they heard a noise – some dogs barking. The dogs soon appeared. There were two of them, and they were friendly, wagging their tails and coming up to be petted.

The dogs began to follow them – and eventually, hoping that the dogs would know the way, David and Judy began to follow the dogs to lower ground. But every once in a while, the dogs would disappear, returning a few moments later to accompany them.

By now Judy was hysterical with fright, and it was all David could do to try to calm her down while still searching for a way out of their predicament.

Finally it was the dogs that led Judy and David back to safe ground near some lighted houses, and at last the two of them felt that they knew their way back to the car.

But they still had a way to go, and their path continued to lead downward. They saw an open drainpipe and decided to follow it down, slipping and sliding along its length.

Every so often David would insist on testing their path before he would let Judy continue on their unsteady journey, as they followed the pipe down to level ground.

Judy was grateful for his concern, and found herself respecting David more than ever. He always thought of *her* welfare first, even though he himself was in as much danger or even more.

When they finally reached the car, which was near the beach, they didn't find Sam and Steve there. So they turned on the headlights to guide the two others back, and then they just waited.

Finally, nearly an hour after David and Judy had arrived back at the car, Sam and Steve came running down the hill, exclaiming: "My God! You guys are alive!"

And David and Judy calmly replied, as though nothing at all had happened: "Yes. Why?"

"Well, we came down here," one of the boys explained, "and you weren't here. Didn't you see? We left weeds on the car to show we'd been here!"

Of course, Judy and David hadn't noticed the weeds. They had been too exhausted to look for any kind of sign – it had never occurred to them to do so.

"No, we didn't notice," David said.

"Well, we thought you and Judy had fallen off the cliff! We didn't know where you were, or anything. . . . We were hysterical! We went up and down the mountain at least three times looking for you."

David looked stunned as he heard this. How could they have missed each other? "You're kidding!" he exclaimed. "We were with the dogs."

"*We* were with the dogs!" the other boys replied almost in unison.

Then the four of them realized that they had never been far apart, though the noise of the surf had drowned out their shouts – and that the dogs had calmly gone back and forth between them, visiting with Sam and Steve and then returning to guide David and Judy.

At this point somebody started to laugh, and the others joined in, thinking of those dogs, who of course had never been lost for one moment . . . and who had managed to lead Judy and David to safety, with time out to see what Sam and Steve were doing a few hundred feet away.

David and Judy patted the dogs affectionately, in grateful farewell. And then the four young people climbed into the car and wearily drove back to Los Angeles.

The night had ended with an unexpectedly comic touch. But tragedy had been hiding somewhere in the darkness, and if it had not been for David's courage and Judy's prayers – and a couple of friendly dogs – they might have faced this tragedy.

*Chapter Thirteen*

# HOW FAME HAS
# CHANGED DAVID

When I first met David Cassidy again at the Bell Records party in 1970 after not seeing him for years, I looked for changes – and they were not hard to find.

Of course he had changed a great deal physically, growing from a very short boy to an adult of medium height. His hair, which had never been long in his early teens, was now shoulder-length.

But the most interesting changes were in his personality. He seemed self-confident and mature, almost sophisticated. And he spoke with a slight trace of a New York accent, which he must have picked up during the several months he spent in New York City while studying and getting his career under way. His attitude toward everyone was friendly but a trifle reserved.

However, I learned later that David's seemingly calm attitude hid a great deal of nervousness over being on public display at a large press party, which the Bell Records affair was. For all this was still very new to him.

Yet everyone seemed to agree that when David was greeting members of the press and other partygoers, he had an amazing amount of self-control.

He was probably helped in this by his New York theatrical experience. Broadway performers are used to coping with stage fright. They know how to turn it into energy that animates their performance, and David's disciplined control of his nerves was similar.

There were more changes as David became a real celebrity. His records became top sellers. *The Partridge*

*Family* rose high in the television ratings. And David's concert appearances, which grossed more than $1,000,000 at the boxoffice in just eight months in 1971, added to his poise and self-confidence. So eventually public appearances became easier for him, and he was much more relaxed.

As we met time and again during the first two years he was on *The Partridge Family*, David seemed to have a growing ability to remove himself mentally from his noisy surroundings on a studio set when he was chatting between takes and concentrate completely on a conversation.

And at home in his beautifully furnished house in the Hollywood Hills, he took obvious pleasure in the luxuries his fame had afforded him. It seemed hard to believe that only a year earlier he had been living contentedly in a tiny apartment in Laurel Canyon with milk crates for chairs. He was indeed a very adaptable person.

He had always enjoyed driving, ever since I had taught him to drive years ago. And the battered Falcon he had owned at the beginning of his first year on *The Partridge Family* soon gave way to better cars, until he had a beautiful new white Corvette in which to drive around town and out to the canyons and the beach.

Yet none of these luxuries seemed to make David conceited or change his essential niceness.

In fact, as I told him one day recently, "David, I frankly like you better now than I used to when you were a kid. Sometimes you could be a real pest in those days. Now you seem a lot pleasanter and more well-adjusted."

He smiled and said, "I guess I've simply grown up."

And that, indeed, seemed to explain it. He had come out of a sometimes frustrated and unhappy adolescence into a life of accomplishment, success and popularity, and he realized that this new life was there to be enjoyed. And enjoy it he did – and still does.

However, his relationships with girls have been complicated by his fame. As he told a mutual friend of ours not long ago, "I'd like nothing better than to get seriously involved with some girl. But I have the same trouble as the Stones!"

In other words, he apparently meant, he shared the problem of the Rolling Stones in finding it difficult to determine whether a girl liked him for himself or for his fame.

And to make things worse, the pressures of his career leave him little time for romance. He is even busier than the Rolling Stones, who don't have a weekly television program to worry about.

Furthermore, unlike the Stones, there is only one of him, and he is under constant public scrutiny. Too close an identification with any one girl, to the point where it looked like a serious romance, might lose him some of his fans – those who wanted to save him for themselves!

But as David had said to me on one occasion, he would not let his fans' attitude toward a girl friend affect any romance or possible marriage if he were really in love. His integrity is too great for it to be any other way. And he trusts that most of his fans would be understanding. At the same time, it can't be too good a feeling – or too conducive to romance – to know that the more deeply you fall in love, the more you risk harming your career.

Also working against marriage in David's mind is the factor of his parents' marital problems. The divorce of his mother and father . . . followed a decade later by the break-up of his mother's marriage to his stepfather, Elliot Silverstein . . . and, in early 1972, the separation of his father, Jack Cassidy, from David's stepmother and co-star, Shirley Jones . . . all these present David with a picture of marriage that makes him feel he wants to be very sure indeed before committing himself to any such arrangement. No wonder he wants to wait a long time before even considering it!

David's devotion to his old friends, as I have often noted, is remarkable. And not only does he enjoy their company – he tries to help them.

He encouraged his roommate, Sam Hyman, in his hopes for a performing career, by involving him in the merchan-

dising of David Cassidy posters and souvenirs at his concerts. And it was David who asked Steve Ross, another old
friend, to be in his back-up group for his concerts, and who
invited Steve to live with him and Sam at their Hollywood
Hills home. Steve took him up on the invitation, and lived
there until he found a place of his own.

And when I kiddingly but truthfully told Dave that I had
been doing very well financially by writing magazine articles
about my interviews and experiences with him, he showed
genuine delight and said, "Great! I want *everybody* to
make money."

On the other hand, David's friends find that he has far
less free time to spend with them now that his daily schedule
is rigidly programmed for him, with script study, rehearsals,
filming, recording, interviews, photography layouts, and
concert tours filling up nearly every available hour from
morning to late at night.

Another change in David's relationship to his friends was
unavoidable. During his early teens, as one of them noted,
he was never really the center of attention in his group. Now
he can't *help* being the center of attention most of the time,
even though he didn't plan it that way.

After all, he generally has to see his friends at his house,
for it's hard to go out in public to the kinds of places he and
they would like to visit without attracting a crowd. So right
away their meetings are on *his* home grounds.

Also, David's friends hold him in such respect for his
achievements that, consciously or unconsciously, they pay a
great deal of attention to what he says and how he reacts to
things.

Yet, at the same time, none of them is afraid to speak to
him frankly about any shortcomings he may have, and certainly no one is afraid to kid him. That's why he cherishes
the friendship of those who "knew him when."

David has become more casual and self-assured about
public appearances at press parties since that Bell Records
party at which we renewed acquaintances. There he wore a

114

coat and tie and neatly pressed slacks – which outfit alone must have been enough to make him a bit uptight, for that is far from being his usual mode of dress. He likes to be very informal in what he wears.

But when the Hollywood Women's Press Club, a very influential group of newswomen, gave David their Golden Apple award recently as the outstanding male newcomer of the year, he appeared at their awards luncheon neatly but informally dressed in a short blue denim jacket, with matching blue jeans and a T shirt.

Although there were many others who dressed with equal informality at the luncheon, since David is a star it was *his* informality that caused comment among some people. Actually, by dressing neatly but in a style which he and his generation prefer, David was letting the others at the lunch see him the way he is, and the way he likes to be. And that in itself was a compliment to them. And in any case, at formal evening occasions, David dresses in a tuxedo and black tie, as befits that particular kind of situation.

All in all, David Cassidy is trying to remain himself amid the many pressures and conflicting influences that he faces in his career and in his life. He is trying to "keep his head together." And the fact that he is succeeding at it so beautifully is a compliment not only to David, but also to his good upbringing, including the good advice he gets from Shirley Jones, who remains a close and trusted friend.

Yes, David has beem changed by fame. He has become a nicer person, and a more self-confident person. Yet he has stayed essentially the same David Cassidy that his friends have always known and liked.

*Chapter Fourteen*

# DAVID GETS
# SOME GOOD ADVICE

As David Cassidy left an exclusive Beverly Hills restaurant one night not long ago, he was upset and embarrassed.

He had just been attending a party in an upstairs banquet room at the restaurant, one of those business parties that he is occasionally obliged to attend as part of his job. And he had not enjoyed it.

For one or two men who had imbibed a bit too much at the party had become unintentionally obnoxious with their rude remarks and thoughtless behavior. And David, who feels a special gallantry toward all women, had considered their inconsiderate actions insulting to the only two ladies present – his stepmother, Shirley Jones, and his date, Judy Strangis, both of whom he had escorted to the party.

His father and Shirley had not yet separated. But that night his dad was busy elsewhere, and that was why David had found himself escorting both Shirley and Judy. So he felt very responsible for both of them, and was disappointed that all had not gone as well as he would have hoped, although nothing serious had occurred.

David didn't want to make a scene at the party, so he waited until he and the two women had left the restaurant before expressing his anger over what had happened.

But when they were all three in the car, David turned to Shirley and exclaimed, "Shirley, I couldn't stand it! Those people were so obnoxious – they were so rowdy!"

But Shirley was philosophical. She had been a star for a long time, and she had learned to cope with embarrassing situations. She listened to David's heated criticisms of the men, and then she shrugged and replied, "That's what you have to go through."

David calmed down a little, but Shirley could see that he was still disturbed. So when the car arrived in front of Shirley's home in Beverly Hills, she didn't get out right away.

In fact, she stayed in the car talking to David for an hour. For she felt that it was time to give her stepson and co-star some advice.

She told him, "Look, David – you have to learn that you can't like all the people with whom you associate. You have to get used to the fact that there are some people who will be obnoxious and rowdy, but this is part of the business. You've just got to be able to handle yourself and let it pass on! It's only going to happen for a few moments."

And then Shirley explained to David that *she* didn't like going to some of the events she had to attend, either. Yet, she noted, she made a point of going to all of them.

David replied: "Shirley, this thing was really for you. All these people were older. These were more *your* fans than they were mine, because they were adults, and they love your work.

"They've seen you. You're a fantastic actress! *You're* the one who should have come to this party, not me. Because I'm just a young kid. But they love your acting, and they all remember you from your movies."

At that point Shirley set David straight.

What she said could only have come from a stepmother who also happened to be David's co-star. And it got to the heart of this unusual relationship of theirs, wherein Shirley is top-billed on their television show, *The Partridge Family*, but is a back-up singer to David on their Bell Records singles and albums despite her marvelous singing voice – a voice which has rated her starring roles in a whole succession of top movie musicals. Her words to David showed the remarkable self-discipline that she brings to her work – and to their relationship.

118

"David, how do you think *I* feel when we have to go on a personal appearance for teenage girls?" she asked him. "Do you think they come to see *me*? No, they come to see *you*! But yet I still have to go to those events, because I am part of *The Partridge Family*.

"Don't you think I feel embarrassed? Those teenage girls don't like *me*. They love *you*. They don't want to see an older woman on the stage.

"And you've got to realize that there are going to be times when it's going to be more *my* audience that we have to see, too," Shirley added. "And you're just going to have to get used to it, just as I have to get used to being with *your* audience."

David took all this in. And when Shirley had finished, he said quietly, "You're right. It's just that it's hard for me to adjust to it now, because it's all new to me, and I'm just beginning to meet people. Before, I never was involved in going to parties and everything. . . ."

And this is true. Even though David's father is Jack Cassidy, David didn't grow up in the Hollywood scene. He didn't go to Hollywood parties and mix with that kind of person. Now he's getting used to it, and it's just been a matter of adjusting.

So he agreed with Shirley about what she had said. He admitted, "Shirley, I guess you're right. How could you stand to go to a concert where all the kids are yelling at Susan Dey and me?"

What Shirley had told David had obviously made a lot of sense to him. He realized after hearing her that everything in his career can't necessarily be the way he wants it to be. He realized that he has to cope with some things he doesn't like.

David's date that evening, Judy Strangis, admires the way Shirley herself coped with the situation at the party. "I love her – she knew how to handle herself so well with those men. She was such a lady through the entire thing!" Judy told me.

Judy has had the opportunity to observe Shirley's behavior on other occasions as well, and has never failed to be impressed. A record awards banquet at the Century Plaza Hotel in 1971, where Shirley and David received a plaque for having the best-selling single of 1970 in Bell Records' *I Think I Love You*, provided another chance for Judy to see Shirley in action. It also provided another lesson for David – this time from his father, Jack Cassidy.

"I was watching Shirley at the banquet," Judy recalls. "People would make jokes, and ... you know how some women will laugh very loudly? Well, Shirley would just smile at all the right things. She was just so *feminine*. That is the perfect word for Shirley Jones – feminine!

"She's a very down-to-earth person, and she's really proud of her three sons – Shaun, Patrick and Ryan. And she seems to take a really big interest in David, even though David is not her real son. She's proud of *him*, too, and I think the advice she is giving him is for his own good.

"Shirley gives David more advice than his father does ... because she *sees* him more than Jack does. His father is in New York so much.

"In fact, at the time of the record awards banquet, his dad had just come back from New York, so David hadn't seen him for several weeks," Judy remembers. "That's why they were in deep conversation for about two hours during the dinner.

"What were they talking about? Well, Neil Diamond was the performer at one point during the banquet, and Jack Cassidy was saying, 'Now, watch, David – he's great! Watch how he comes on, and how he talks, and how he conducts himself.'

"You see, this was about two weeks before David's first concert, and David was getting very nervous about it," Judy explained. "So during Neil Diamond's whole performance, Jack was saying, "See, David, see what Neil Diamond is doing?' David didn't say much – because he was listening to what his father was saying. And David liked the performance."

David also listened to his father's comments about his own behavior at the banquet. His father felt that David should have made a longer acceptance speech. David had merely said 'Thank you' and had then turned the microphone over to Shirley. Again, hearing his father criticize him for this, David was respectful of his dad's advice and took it all in.

Judy explains, however, that David actually hadn't known about the awared in advance. Shirley and Jack had known about it, but they had wanted it to be a surprise to David, apparently – and it was! That was why he had no speech prepared.

"David actually didn't know that he had the biggest-selling single of 1970," Judy marvels. "He doesn't look at the record charts a lot of the time. And he doesn't see most of the publicity about him in all the magazines."

However, David's conversations with Jack Cassidy and Shirley Jones don't consist only of getting advice. At the awards, Shirley had on a beautiful dress by the noted designer, Geoffrey Beene. Seeing it, David told her, "You look *great* tonight! Where did you get that dress?"

And Shirley replied, "Your father bought it for me for our anniversary."

David looked in amazement at Jack Cassidy and said, "Dad, how in the world did you know how to pick out the right dress for Shirley?'

Jack explained, "When you get to know a woman well, you kind of know what she looks good in and what her taste is." And then he added, "Wouldn't you know how to pick out something for Judy?"

David quietly admitted, "No – I don't know *anything* about ladies' clothes! And when I'm with Judy, she's never the same. She always has something different on." But David obviously was proud to know that his father had picked out Shirley's beautiful dress.

So there's much good-humored banter between David and his father ... and between David and Shirley, to whom he has been close for years. It isn't always lesson time, by any means. Yet David respects both Jack and Shirley so much that he doesn't mind it when they do give him advice.

It's a good thing David *doesn't* mind it. For, as Judy Strangis told me, "I think Shirley and Jack seem to give David advice and put him down on occasion so that all his success won't go to his head.

"A lot of parents will always say, 'Congratulations – you did so well!' But basically, when I hear Shirley or Jack giving David an opinion, it's mainly criticism – telling him what he should do and what he shouldn't, what he didn't do and so on.

"Thanks in part to them, David's fame has *not* gone to his head," Judy notes happily. "To him, his success is like a big dream! He was in a state of shock when he learned that *I Think I Love You* had sold a million copies." (The final total was several times that.)

Judy feels that David is particularly lucky to have someone like Shirley Jones to talk to him, criticize him and give him advice. "Sometimes you can talk more easily to someone of the opposite sex – and someone who isn't actually your own parent," she noted.

But more than that, it is Shirley's own unique qualities that make her such a useful confidante and adviser for David, Judy believes. "David told me, 'She's really great – a great lady! She's one in a million.' And I agree.

"Yes, Shirley is a very good influence on David, because she's a very smart person," Judy concluded. "She really knows where it's at!"

## Chapter Fifteen

## ... AND QUICK DEATH
## COULD HAVE FOLLOWED

The pain exploded in the early hours of July 12, 1971, while David Cassidy was sleeping – a horrible pain that made him wonder if he was going to die. He woke up screaming.

Terrified, he tried to rise, but the pain made him double over helplessly.

His roommate, Sam Hyman, heard his screams and came running from his own bedroom to see what was the matter.

David knew what the trouble was. For he had felt this same kind of pain just two weeks earlier. Then, too, it had made him scream and cry, until a doctor had hurried over to the big house in the Hollywood Hills and given him a dose of morphine. The morphine had ended his agony for awhile. But now it was back, worse than ever.

The doctor had told David that he was suffering from gall bladder trouble. Gallstones had formed and were causing the intense pain.

The news was no real surprise to David. For he had been suffering from several abdominal pains off and on since the age of 14 – something highly unusual for so young a person.

David is a bit moody today, and he was even moodier then, I remember. And underneath the moodiness of the 14-year-old David Cassidy there was apparently also a certain amount of underlying tension. For that was when he first thought that he had an ulcer.

Actually, he now remembers, it *was* the beginnings of an ulcer. But early and effective treatment prevented the ulcer from actually forming.

However, there was another cause for the pains he felt from time to time. For David had already begun to suffer from the gall bladder trouble that would become so serious by the time he was 21.

I don't recall his having been on any particular stringent diet in his early teens, either for the incipient ulcer or for the gall bladder pains. And indeed he never mentioned these problems to me at the time.

As I remember, he was a typical teenage ice-box raider, eating any food that might be at hand. And he never missed a chance to enjoy hamburgers at some burger stand, according to his friends.

But, although he generally didn't complain about it except to his mother, David was already suffering from damage to his gall bladder. So he had to endure occasional pain and digestive upsets.

For several years, David's gall bladder trouble was treated with medicine, in hopes that an operation might be avoided. He led an active life, enjoying surfing, hiking and other sports – including, most recently, scuba diving.

Indeed, if he hadn't been stricken with the illness himself, David might have gone through life knowing little or nothing about the gall bladder, a sac attached to the liver in which excess gall, also known as bile, is stored until needed.

The gall bladder aids the stomach in the absorption and digestion of fats. When pebbles called gallstones form, they interfere with the function of the gall bladder and can cause tremendous pain, as eventually happened in David's case.

After his first major attack, which took place at the beginning of July, 1971, his doctor had told David that he would have to have an operation.

But since it would take him weeks to recover from surgery, David elected to wait six months until January, 1972, when filming on his ABC-TV series, *The Partridge Family*, would be over for the season.

After all, he had so much going for him, and, with it all, so many obligations. Not only was the TV series a hit – a hit that kept him working five days a week, from early morning to early evening – he also had to record songs frequently, not only for the show but for release as records, which became instant hits.

His gold records in turn had led to a series of tremendously successful concerts, and David's weekends were usually taken up with flying all over the country for concert dates, often two in a weekend in different cities.

As a result of all this activity, David's eating habits were far from the best.

Lunch often had to be eaten while simultaneously doing a publicity interview in some crowded, noisy restaurant near the Screen Gems ranch in Burbank, where *The Partridge Family* was being filmed.

Dinner at home with his roommate, Sam Hyman, was often a catch-as-catch-can affair, and was sometimes rushed. For David often had to spend his evenings in the recording studio after the day's filming, since there was no other time when he could cut his records.

Flying cross-country in jets for his concerts, his mealtimes became completely mixed up, what with the time changes and the pressures of preparing concerts in strange auditoriums.

Someone with gall bladder trouble should not eat in the haphazard way that David was eating. But there was so much to do, and so little time to do it, that something had to suffer. And too often it was David's diet. So it is not surprising that his already impaired digestive system could not cope with the added strains on it.

Gradually the pain from his gall bladder, which had been relatively mild in the past, began to increase alarmingly. And the results soon showed.

Fellow cast members and visitors to the set of *The Part-*

*ridge Family* sometimes commented on the fact that David could be cheerful and joking one minute, and then would suddenly take on a moody, faraway look. When they learned later of the pains he had been suffering for years, pains which became much worse as the strains on him mounted, this sudden change of mood seemed more understandable.

But he had not talked much about the pains until the first bad attack. And then, knowing that he would soon have to have a gall bladder operation, not only was he willing to talk about it, but he also wanted to know everything he could about such operations.

On July 4, 1971, only two days after that first seizure – which had forced him to miss a day's work on *The Partridge Family* – David had felt well enough to attend an informal get-together at co-star Dave Madden's home in Malibu with his date, Judy Strangis. In talking to the other guests, he learned that one man had also suffered from gallstones and had been forced to have his gall bladder removed.

David questioned the man anxiously, trying to find out as much as he could about the operation. What he heard was not too pleasant.

And he could only agree when the man commented on how terrible his gall bladder pains had been before the operation. Someone even compared them to the pain of having a baby by natural childbirth. And it was agreed that nobody could think of a worse pain than that caused by the gallstones.

The man even showed David his surgical scar. Although the operation had taken place three years earlier, the scar was still red and vivid. It was a frightening sight.

David cringed, and suddenly exclaimed: "I don't want to have this operation. It's going to be the *worst*! No, I've really got to watch myself, because I definitely don't want to ever have to have an operation."

And that day at Malibu he did watch his diet carefully.

All the other guests were enjoying hot dogs and similar picnic fare, but David asked if he could have some tuna fish and tomatoes. They had to make a trip to the market to get the food for him, but Madden was glad to oblige, for he was concerned about David's health – although, as he would tell me later, he had no idea how serious his condition would become.

Despite his vow at the party to try to avoid the operation, David must have known in his heart that this would not be possible. Yet he did continue in his resolution to postpone it until January – although if necessary it could be moved up to August, when the cast of *The Partridge Family* would take a short hiatus after completing the first several episodes for the 1971–72 television season.

David wanted to postpone the surgery not only because of his TV series, but also because most of his weekends for months ahead were already slated to be filled with concert appearances. He knew it was important to do these concerts while his popularity and that of the show were at their peak.

For he realized all too well that teenage idols are idolized with such intensity for only a relatively short time, usually just two or three years.

So it only made good sense to utilize his popularity fully at a time when he was on the cover of every teenage magazine being published. That was one reason why he did not want to cancel any of his scheduled concerts if at all possible.

But there was another reason, too, and it was very important to David. From his mail, he knew how eagerly his fans all over the country were looking forward to seeing him in person in their own home towns. He was sincerely touched by their devotion, and he couldn't bear to let his fans down, despite the risk to his health which was involved.

Indeed, he had done a concert in New Jersey the same weekend he had his second bad attack. On Saturday morning at 7:30, a car had come to his house to pick him up and take him to the Los Angeles airport. He had flown to New Jersey accompanied by his roommate, Sam, who was handling the program and souvenir concessions for his concerts, and by his regular back-up musicians – all of them his friends.

David and Sam had arrived back home on Sunday afternoon, and David had gone to bed early, for by then he wasn't feeling at all well.

It was three o'clock Monday morning when David's agonized screams woke Sam and brought him running into the room. With Sam helping him, David telephoned his mother, who had only recently moved back to California from the East.

She promised to come right over. She had been staying at David's house when he had his first attack, but she was now living in her own place in nearby Brentwood. The doctor was called again, and once more he hurried over to ease David's pain.

But David couldn't sleep any more that night. Nor could the doctor permit him any more delays in seeking a permanent cure for his ailment. Along with David's mother, he insisted that David go to Mt. Sinai Hospital for tests.

That same afternoon, July 12th, David checked into Mt. Sinai, having been taken there by his mother, personal manager Ruth Aarons, and his publicist, Jim Flood (who would later join the Aarons office as David's personal manager and press agent.)

They arrived at the hospital shortly after one o'clock. David checked into a private room and the tests began. At 5:45 p.m. that same day David's doctor entered his hospital room and informed David and his mother that it would be necessary to remove the ailing gall bladder the very next morning. For infection had already set in, and there was no time for delay.

David's response was odd, almost funny. Although he had seen a gall bladder operation scar only a week before,

128

when the doctor told him that his own gall bladder would have to be removed his reply was a question: "Where is it?"

Perhaps he was trying to make a joke to relieve the tension of this serious moment. Or perhaps his mind had succeeded in blotting out the memory of that ugly scar. . . .

Jack Cassidy and Shirley Jones had been kept informed, of course. David wanted them to know everything. And Shirley had made a gracious gesture. She offered the use of her home for David's recovery.

Grateful as he was for her kindness, David declined the offer, for his own home was ample. Yet he was impressed once more by her thoughtfulness. He realized anew that she was much more to him than a stepmother, more than a co-star. She was his friend and trusted confidante, someone to whom he could talk more easily than to his father because she was gentler and more understanding, although he loved his father dearly.

On the day of David's operation, a strange sight and a very touching one could be seen in a waiting room near Surgery at Mt. Sinai Hospital. Two women, who by nature should perhaps have been rivals, comforted each other as they waited for word of the success or failure of the operation.

Shirley Jones – still young and beautiful in her middle 30s, her blonde hair curling softly about her doll-like face with its large blue eyes. The woman who had married David's father in 1956, almost immediately after Jack Cassidy's divorce from the other woman in the room – David's mother, Evelyn.

Evelyn – a bit older, but beautiful in her own exotic way, her darker hair and slightly slanted eyes showing her to be David's mother, even though David's own eyes are fuller and wider than hers. For David is a perfect cross between his mother and father in appearance.

Jack Cassidy was there with Shirley soon after David was admitted to the hospital.

While the doctor operated, David's mother and step-mother prayed, united in a sudden comradeship that transcended the problems of the past, their thoughts only of David.

But if one woman suffered more, it was Evelyn. For Shirley had her husband and three handsome young sons, but Evelyn had only David. He was her whole life now, and she couldn't bear to think of losing him.

Finally the doctor came in and reassured the two women. The operation was over, and it had been a success. Although David was under intensive care at the moment, he would be all right.

And, yet, it had been a near-tragedy. One physician said of David's case, "He could have had peritonitis. It could have gone quickly into peritonitis and death. . . ."

Even after the operation, there was much misery still to come for David Cassidy on the long road to recovery. He doesn't remember much about the four or five days immediately after the operation, except that he was fed intravenously, with a tube coming into his nose and another going out of his side. And yet, says David, although he was very uncomfortable for days, the sedatives and pain killers prevented his feeling any really intense pain. The operation had ended that kind of pain for him.

David was in the hospital for two weeks. At first he could have no visitors other than members of his family, nor could friends telephone his room. But eventually they were able to phone him by using a special code to get through. This was necessary, for the hospital switchboard had been deluged by calls from fans and journalists from all over the country and abroad. Of course, none of these people could get through, with David in the condition that he was. But when he learned about all the calls from his fans, he was deeply touched – as he was touched by the gifts that flooded the hospital for him, gifts of all kinds from his admirers. There were more, actually, than he could possibly use, so most of them were donated by David to the children who were confined to the hospital.

David loves children, and was delighted when his 12-year-old half-brother, Shaun, came to the hospital one day to visit him. The two of them have long been good friends. His two younger half-brothers, Patrick and Ryan, were not old enough to be allowed in, however.

When Shirley brought Shaun to the hospital, she had to run a gauntlet of worried fans who were waiting outside, many of them eager to press notes and gifts on her for delivery to David. A few overly eager individuals even attempted to get to David's room to see him, and a guard had to be posted at his door to keep intruders out while David lay ill.

Don Rickles, the insult comedian, was recuperating in the same hospital from an operation for a severed Achiles tendon – the result of a tennis accident. Don cheered David by assuring him that he needn't worry about not being able to produce any gall. Don himself would produce enough for both of them, he assured David.

Soon David felt well enough to start phoning his closest friends. One of them was Judy Strangis, who remembers, "He sounded weak on the phone, but pretty good. The first time he called me I was completely shocked.

"I said, 'My God, you're calling. I thought you were on your deathbed!' In fact, when I first picked up the phone and he said, 'Hello, Judy, this is David,' I said, 'David? David who?' Because I had heard that nobody could talk to him yet. He called me a few times more from the hospital, wanting to know what was happening and telling me when he'd be home."

During one of these calls, Judy told David, "Well, I guess you're going to have to cancel your concerts."

And David said with determination, "The one concert I *can't* cancel is the one in New Jersey on August 14th." This concert, slated for the Garden State Arts Center, had been an immediate sellout, and a matinee performance had been added to the schedule to handle the overflow.

Since David had spent so much of his childhood in New

Jersey, living with his mother and grandparents, he had fond memories of his early years there and did not want to disappoint his fans there by canceling his appearances. His only concession to his recent surgery, he told Judy, would be to tone down some of his more strenuous movements around the stage.

Judy was startled when David told her, "Maybe I'll drive over and see you on my way home from the hospital."

"*Drive* over?" she asked. "Aren't you going to be in bed?"

"No, that's why they're keeping me in the hospital – so that when I go home I won't be bedridden," David explained.

As it turned out, Judy had to tell David not to bother to come over on his way home, because she had to work that day on her TV series, *Room 222*. But plenty of friends flocked to David's big house in the Hollywood Hills to welcome him home from the hospital. And most of them were old pals from his teenage days in Westwood.

On August ninth, less than a month after the attack that had sent him to the hospital, David Cassidy capped an amazingly fast recovery by returning to work on *The Partridge Family*.

There was no big welcome-back celebration – there wasn't time. The show was a week and a half behind schedule because of his illness and operation, and the script featured lots of action that kept most of the cast very busy.

Fortunately the action focused on the younger children, allowing David plenty of time to get back into the swing of things. Whenever he felt that he needed a rest, he would ask for some time off to go to his dressing room and lie down.

And at lunch time he would eat just a little bit and then spend an hour napping.

Nevertheless, he still wanted to gain weight. For his weight loss because of the surgery and the intravenous feeding had shocked him when he first saw his face in a mirror at the hospital, and it was still noticeable. To his chagrin, he found that the pants he had previously worn for his role in *The Partridge Family* no longer fitted him. They had to send out for several new pairs of pants in a smaller size. The main thing that bothered David about being thinner was that he thought it made him look even younger than he had previously, and he has always looked young for his age.

Although David found himself tiring easily during his first week back on the show, he was still determined to go through with the two New Jersey concerts. And he did – to the frenzied applause and cheers of his fans, who knew that little more than two weeks earlier he had been in the hospital.

Following these concerts, David returned to Hollywood and an even more strenuous schedule. For his second week back on the show found him recording in the evenings, on top of filming all day.

His friends worried that he might over-exert himself. But to David, this was his life and he loved it. It was the weeks of forced inactivity during his illness that he hadn't liked. And he was glad to be back at work. Even the prospect of six solid weeks of weekend concerts following his New Jersey triumph did not faze him, and he got through them all successfully.

He couldn't bear to let his fans down – even if it meant working literally night and day. For he knew how much they wanted to see and hear him. And, more than ever before, he knew how much he wanted to be with *them*. For he would never forget the outpourings of their devotion while he had been in the hospital, recovering from surgery and the illness that had almost cost him his life.

*Chapter Sixteen*

# A CO-STAR LOOKS
## AT DAVID CASSIDY

What's it like to work with David Cassidy on *The Partridge Family*? His co-star, Dave Madden, knows. And Dave – a wry and witty man who plays Reuben Kincaid, the family's manager, on the popular ABC-TV series – told me all about it during a recent lunch at a restaurant near the Screen Gems ranch.

"How do you enjoy working on the show?" I asked Dave.

"I enjoy it very much!" he assured me. "It's a show that makes me enjoy getting up and going to work. And anything that makes me enjoy getting up in the morning has *got* to be fun!"

"What do you like about it?" I wanted to know.

"For one thing," he pointed out, "it's a *harmonious* set. If there were friction on the set, that would kill it for me instantly. But there isn't. There isn't friction among the cast, among the crew, or between the cast and crew, and that makes it a very pleasant set to work on."

"Was there friction on the set when you were starring on *Rowan and Martin's Laugh-In*?" I asked him, having read newspaper accounts of various tensions on that show.

"Rarely did it come out on the surface," he recalled. "But there were always *undercurrents* of things that were going on." He grinned and noted, "It was always Rumor Junction around the *Laugh-In* set! Things supposedly were happening, or were going to happen.

"But then," he pointed out, "you had a great many people there with diverse backgrounds and personalities. There were *bound* to be some clashes in that kind of a

135

situation. But they were very rarely brought out onto the set or into rehearsal halls or any place like that. Occasional snide remarks were about as much as you'd ever hear."

"What is the atmosphere on *The Partridge Family* compared to *Laugh-In*? Are the people on the set more chummy? More aloof?" I asked him.

"On *Laugh-In* there were a lot more people my own age that I worked with," Dave noted. "Our senses of humor were similar. We were doing similar things, in terms of the kind of comedy presented on the show."

And then he added, with a gentle grin, "You can't say that there's any similarity on this show between what I'm doing and what the little girl, Suzanne Crough, is doing. Is there any similarity between what I'm doing and what David Cassidy is doing? There's none! There's no similarity between what I'm doing and what Shirley Jones is doing, except that we both happen to be adults. But I'm not saying that isn't good."

"You each have a showcase for your individual talents that way, I observed. "But is it kind of lonely for you?"

"Yes – that's the whole point. There were more people to relate to on *Laugh-In*. So, in terms of pure fun, being on *The Partridge Family* is not as much *fun*. But it's more rewarding."

"Who are your best friends on the *Partridge Family* set?" I asked.

Dave, who is of a rather precise and philosophical bent, pondered that question for a moment before answering, "I've always found it difficult to draw a line between *friends* and associates and acquaintances."

"Are they all your associates, then?"

"Yes, they are . . . and acquaintances, of course . . . certainly *acquaintances*. But *friends*? I only have maybe two or three. One of them is in the business. The other two aren't."

Obviously, then, Dave seems to regard his fellow actors on *The Partridge Family* as pleasant, compatible acquaintances, rather than close friends. And I had noted that most of the cast members went their own ways between takes and upon leaving work, which is not necessarily a bad thing when people are thrown together day after day who really have little in common at all. It probably contributes a great deal, in fact, to the harmonious atmosphere that exists on the set, for they don't get tired of each other or grate on each other's nerves.

Dave seemed in a way to confirm this as he reiterated, "But it's a very pleasant set to work on. And from time to time the things you have to do present a challenge to you as a performer, which makes it interesting. I guess those are the main reasons why I enjoy it."

"Have there been any changes around the set since the first year of the show?" I asked David.

"Well, David Cassidy is doing a lot of concerts that he wasn't doing at the beginning," Dave noted, "and I imagine it wears him out. Because he's not getting proper rest. On the other hand, one would assume he's getting wealthy at it!"

He smiled as he added, "I certainly wouldn't say that if *I* were David Cassidy and I had the opportunity to go out and make that kind of money on weekends, that I wouldn't be doing it. I guess *everybody* would. *I* would because I have a greedy manager who loves money – which is fortunate for me!"

"What's it like, being on a show with a reigning teenage idol?" I wondered. "Has all that adulation affected David much, in your opinion?"

"Oh, not to any great extent. Not to the extent that one would *expect* it to affect a young man who was suddenly thrown from semi-oblivion into national or *international* fame. I suspect that one of the reasons that he's been able to cope with it as well as he has is because he comes from a show business family," Dave observed.

"If I, at the age of 19, 20 or 21, had been thrown out of North Terre Haute, Indiana, into that kind of fame and

137

fortune," he admitted, "I don't know *what* it would have done to *my* character and personality ... because that would have been too startling a change!

"But David seems to be handling it very well, as far as I can see. I know that in terms of *our* relationship, such as it is, it has not floundered or fallen apart or changed in any sense. And I'm sure that if he had become a Big Star around the set, it *would* have changed...."

"What is your relationship right now?"

"Well, it's a difficult thing to put into words, or even understand, I guess. It certainly is not a father-son image. It might come closer to being an older brother kind of relationship at times. But, to be as specific as one could, it's a *friend* relationship, with one of us being older than the other," Dave said, apparently forgetting for the moment that he had implied all his fellow performers on the show were merely acquaintances rather than friends.

"I have never had any father-son talks with him," he emphasized. "I've never given him advice on anything unless he asked for it. Because, there again, I consider anything in terms of his personal life as something I have no business being involved in ... and, in terms of his professional life, he has managers, agents and all sorts of people running *that* for him."

He smiled. "So our relationship, generally speaking, is of a much more frivolous nature. It rarely gets terribly serious.

"Occasionally we may get in an argument about rock 'n' roll music or something. I like to tease David occasionally about rock music and some of the forms that it takes – the lyrics. Not rock music relative to *The Partridge Family*, which I find the least offensive and the most tolerable to my taste of any rock music that I've heard – it's very soft and it's nice, most of it, and I enjoy it.

"But that stuff that goes into the category of hard or acid rock to me is just *in*tolerable!" he confessed.

"Yet that's what David likes," I noted.

"Yes, he seems to – and that's an area where I could *never* come to an understanding with him. There's *no* line of communication there. He obviously grew up with that kind of music. I grew up struggling with it, and he grew up accepting it because of his particular age group that accepted it.

"But when somebody who likes Nat King Cole starts talking to somebody who likes Janis Joplin," Dave summed up helplessly, "there's just no area for discussion. It's like discussing religion!"

Ironically, in the two areas in which they share common interests – scuba diving and photography – the two Daves don't seem to have found time to explore their hobbies together.

"Have you and David gone skin diving together yet?" I asked. "You mentioned to me once that you were planning to."

"No, we haven't," he admitted. "Maybe we'll work it out during our next hiatus."

He also failed to make any mention of David Cassidy's new hobby, photography, while telling me of his own interest in the subject.

"Photography takes a lot of my spare time," he noted. "I photograph *people*, mostly. I shoot pictures of the crew and of our directors and guest stars, but only a few of the regulars on our show. If I really wanted pictures of the cast, I'd just go to them and ask them for one!

"But I *have* shot pictures of Susan Dey, Shirley Jones, Danny Bonaduce . . . and I took one of David Cassidy which I had blown up and gave to him. Generally speaking, though, I don't photograph our cast."

"Do you socialize with any of the cast members?" I asked him. Not surprisingly, his answer was in the negative.

"No, not really. Not too much," he confessed. "Shirley, of course, has a family, has her own life. Socializing with Shirley Jones doesn't make any sense whatsoever.

"David is a younger man. He has his own group of friends, and is doing concerts and things like that. So there's not that much of an opportunity to socialize with David. And Susan Dey is a little young for me. The younger kids do come out sometimes to visit me at the beach, but that's about the degree of socializing."

"That reminds me . . . I hear you had a big party on the Fourth of July just before David Cassidy's operation in 1971, and that David attended," I told him.

"Yes, we had quite a few people out, but I don't like to think of it as a party," he said. "I don't *like* parties!"

"Well, what was your splash-in or non-party like?" I persisted.

"It was just a day at the beach. We went out and built a fire on the beach and shot off some fireworks that evening. But it wasn't a planned party. I just invite people out occasionally, or they drop by. David and Susan and Danny Bonaduce were there – I guess that's all from the cast."

Such rare occasions aside, the cast members on *The Partridge Family* don't tend to get together for rap sessions, even on the set.

"It's just that life on the set is so *segmented*," Dave explained. "You sit down and start talking, and that silly air horn blasts out to indicate that filming is starting and we have to be silent. And one or both of us have to walk on the set and shoot the shot for this angle or stand off-camera for that one. And it goes like that continuously. They don't leave you alone long enough to really *talk* about anything. There's always somebody who has to jump up and do something . . . go to the phone or change or go on the set or something like that.

"And then, during lunch periods, Shirley usually has lunch in her dressing room. She usually has visitors, or maybe interviews, and then when the day is over she splits. And the others also go their own ways, at lunch and after work. Even with Shirley, who's in my age group, I can't say

140

that I have ever really had a deep discussion about anything, for that matter. I don't even know how much we have in common. There's never been a chance to really find out!"

"Were there any problems when David got sick in the summer of 1971 and had to have his gall bladder removed?" I asked Madden. His casual answers to my questions on the subject surprised me – until I realized that David so successfully hid his suffering and the seriousness of the operation from his fellow workers (except for Shirley Jones, of course) that most of them never realized the gravity of his illness.

"No, the problem was just that we broke for a month," Dave said – and added wryly: "If you consider *that* a problem, there was a big one!" For television filming schedules are very tightly organized, and are planned far in advance in order to meet broadcast deadlines.

"Was there much worry about it?" I asked.

"You mean, 'Will we catch up and when will we get started again?' Not really, because we had planned a month's hiatus to start about a month later, anyway. So our month's hiatus just came a month earlier than planned, that was all."

"Was there much worry about *David*?" I said, clarifying my question.

"I don't think ... you mean for his life – and limbs? I worried about his gall bladder. You know – who was going to get it! I was hoping that he'd give it to *me*," Dave said with an engaging grin. "No, I don't think that anybody thought it was so desperately serious that he was in danger. Maybe his mother did. Maybe they knew something I didn't. All I knew was that he had a gall bladder attack and had to have the gall bladder taken out."

He had turned more serious, but now he smiled again as he revealed, "I kidded David a lot before the operation – I had him worried for a while!

"Because I told him, 'Well, you know when the gall bladder comes out, it throws the metabolism out of balance. Medically, it has to happen to you, because it's happened to everybody who's ever had his gall bladder taken out: You will gain between 30 and 40 pounds!'

"I said, 'There is a chance, with proper diet and exercise, you might lose 10 or 15 of that. But you might as well resign yourself that you're going to be 20 or 25 pounds heavier than you are now for the rest of your life.'

"I told him this straight-faced, you know," Dave added mischievously, "and he was really concerned. I let him go for about half a day with this. Then I told him the truth.

"He's like Susan Dey, because he couldn't bear to gain more than a pound and a half. They don't know what weight problems are," Dave assured me. And then he sighed. "And, God, I hope they never find out!"

Our conversation turned to what the future holds for David and the cast of *The Partridge Family* and for the show itself.

"It'll be interesting to see if David Cassidy's right, that the show does run five or six years," Madden observed. "It'll be interesting to see what will happen with these kids, because they really *are* in that growing stage, and see the difference in the look of the group, for example, as these kids get older.

"It's hard for me to envision, five or six years from now, watching the Partridge Family on a set, performing a musical number. I can't envision that!" he admitted.

"Suppose they marry off Shirley on the show?" I suggested.

"Well, that becomes a problem overwrought with problems," Dave said skeptically, "marrying off Shirley and continuing *The Partridge Family*. They may marry off Susan Dey by then. But would Shirley marry some guy that's going to ride on the Partridge Family bus and not do anything for a living? I just don't see how they could fit that in."

Then we began to talk about the ups and downs of success as they have related to Dave Madden, and as they may relate to David Cassidy tomorrow. What Madden said about his experiences with fame – and with the occasional disappearance or decline of fame – was something that should be of interest to David and all young performers, as well as those who *aspire* to show business success.

It began when I asked Madden, "Has the success of *The Partridge Family* on television affected you much? Are you recognized more?"

"No, my career for the past five or six years has been up and down in that respect," he observed. "When I was on the *Camp Runamuck* series, although it was a losing show I got the first taste of what it was like to be recognized.

"Then the *Runamuck* show went down the drain after a year, and I saw what it was like to have fewer and fewer people know who you are.

"Then I had the *Laugh-In* series and got to know what *real* fame was like. Then that petered out. Then I had this.

"So the recognition bit is not where it's at – not what's important. Probably one of the first disillusioning factors of being in this business is involved with that. The first year, you think: 'Fame! Wouldn't it be wonderful if they recognized me?' Then you find that fame is a prison that locks you into only being able to go certain places and do certain things comfortably. It restricts the world in which you can move when you're famous. And though it's nice for a while, it can get to be a pain in the neck!

"And once you find that out, then that aspect of it doesn't mean that much to you anymore. *Then* you start thinking of more serious things than the dream of fame ... things like doing what you do a little better than you do it now ... things that are esthetically of a little more importance to you than the frivolous things, fame and fortune."

"His fame certainly restricts David now," I observed. "Did he ever comment on that?"

"Yeah, he has commented on it," Madden said. "I suspect that he sometimes tends to exaggerate to what degree he can go anywhere and do anything.

"I imagine that if David wanted to go out to Disneyland and put on a floppy hat and a pair of sunglasses and a pair of overalls and a camera around his neck, and wander around Disneyland taking pictures, that he'd probably go into total shock over the fact that not very many people, if anybody, would recognize him!

"David Cassidy in the world of adults is not that noticeable. If he goes into a popular spot for a hamburger, you might have some problems, however. If he comes into this delicatessen, or that restaurant across the street, he hasn't got any problems. Is he going to be disturbed? Of course not.

"So where do his problems lie, in terms of not being able to go anywhere? He can't go undisguised, blatantly, into places where young people hang out. *That's* where he can't go. Logically, that makes sense, right? But I think in his imagination he is more restricted than he is in reality.

"He has probably had some bad experiences that make him believe that he can't go anywhere now," Madden admitted. "And I don't think that's really true."

"He did have that bad experience at Marineland where he was chased into the men's room and the girls followed him in," I said, and we both smiled at the thought.

But Madden was not dissuaded from his viewpoint. "Well, in a place like Marineland, especially when you go to Marineland to shoot a television film, there's a little difference between that and just going to *visit* Marineland."

"What did David say about that experience?" I asked him.

"Oh, I haven't heard him dwell on it. He just says it's a very difficult thing to go anywhere," Madden replied.

"But I think he enjoys his fame," I observed, and Madden agreed.

"He would be a little strange if he didn't enjoy it to *some* degree. I don't know. I suspect that to whatever degree you
144

really enjoy recognition, you'll never really find out until the recognition starts to fade. Then, no matter what you tell yourself, *that* is when you find out how important it was to you. Because if you can see it fading and it really doesn't matter, then you're kind of over the hump."

"After *Camp Runamuck* ended, did you miss being recognized at first?" I asked him.

"Yeah, in strange ways that I can't describe it *was* disturbing to a degree. Because I guess that what you related it to was your career slipping. And I don't know if that was a logical reference to make, necessarily – your career slipping because there are less people recognizing who you are.

"But the main thing about it is that you learn very quickly not to take it all very seriously, and not let it overwhelm you, and not let the public's opinion of you or adulation of you suddenly take on the aspect of your thinking that you're really as great as they seem to *think* you are.

"You've got to know that a year or two years from now, they won't know who you are. You'll hear people say things like, 'Wasn't that David Cassidy?' And the word *wasn't* is a little frightening!"

I told Madden, "I think David himself talks in terms of it lasting only two or three years, this matter of being a teenage idol. He seems to be quite conscious of that."

Dave nodded approvingly. "I think he is – again, because he has been raised in an atmosphere of show business, and he has *had* to see it happen in the lives of other people.

"And he has to know that it can happen to him. 'Not that it necessarily *will*, but that it *can* happen to him. It can happen to anybody!" he concluded.

Thoughtful words, those, from Dave Madden – a man of wit and wisdom who chooses words carefully. David Cassidy is lucky to have him as a friend, acquaintance, or whatever Madden chooses to call it.

It's only a shame that the pressures of their work don't allow them more time to talk together. But at least, when

145

David reads this chapter, he and Madden will have had this one serious rap session – even if it took place within the pages of a book!

*Chapter Seventeen*

# DAVID IS
# ROBBED IN EUROPE

At the end of 1971, an exhausted David Cassidy finally managed to get away on his first long vacation since attaining stardom. And he really needed it. Or, as he himself put it shortly before leaving, "I can't wait. I'm just so tired!"

Just after Christmas, David flew to Europe for a five-week stay, and he confided to friends that he was going *alone*.

This in itself was a drastic change in his life style. For David Cassidy had never really been alone before.

He had always lived either with family members or roommates. And during his years on *The Partridge Family*, as his fame grew, so did the number of people around him ... people who worked either with or for him to advance his thriving career.

"He's constantly surrounded by many people," observed one of the people who constantly surrounded him. And it was true. Production executives, recording people, wardrobe men, makeup men, directors, chauffeurs for concert trips, and, finally, guards to protect him from the crowds that sometimes seemed about to overwhelm him during public appearances – all these well-intentioned people left him almost no time to himself, even though each of them was necessary to his work and way of life.

But when David was finally away from all these people – when he arrived in romantic Rome on the very first day of his European vacation, exactly the same thing happened to him that had occurred when he had tried "getting away from it all" once before by moving from his besieged Laurel Canyon pad to a Hollywood Hills hideaway.

He was robbed.

It seemed that he couldn't run away after all – even if he fled all the way to Europe!

For the camper van he had just picked up in Rome, which he intended to drive around Europe, was broken into that same day while he was away from it for a short while.

His passport was stolen. So was his international driver's license. And so were nearly $1,000 worth of traveller's checks. All were replaced with no financial loss, but the theft caused annoying delays – and it got his European vacation off to an unpleasant start, just as he thought he had found a bit of relaxation at last.

But finally he got everything squared away and left Rome behind him, as he drove his camper van through Italy and any other countries he felt like visiting on the spur of the moment. There was nobody to tell him what to do, no assistant director calling him to the set, no answering service to wake him with a call that meant he was off to another concert appearance.

It was heaven. And it was his for a month. Not until February, when he had promised to make an appearance to promote his Bell Records releases in London, did he have any professional commitments at all. Jim Flood was flying to England to meet him for the February appearance, but until then he was on his own.

Yet he had to keep his associates back in Hollywood informed of his whereabouts from time to time, so they wouldn't worry about him and could reach him in an emergency. And the European public was well aware of who David Cassidy was, for *The Partridge Family* is seen in 32 countries around the world. So his privacy was not complete. But he was alone far more than he ever could be in Hollywood, and he loved it.

Driving through the European cities and countryside, David had time at last to think of all the amazing things that had happened to him in the past few years, and to ponder what he wanted to do in the future.

He was determined to get into the writing and performing

of heavier music, more in the direction of such greats as George Harrison as far as quality was concerned – but with a style of his own. His advisers were already looking for a suitable motion picture script for his movie debut, for he wanted to be a serious actor, while continuing with his singing and composing.

Money would not be a problem for the foreseeable future. His records were all hits, beginning with his very first, *I Think I Love You*, which had sold 5,000,000 copies. His concerts packed them in, and *The Partridge Family* seemed to be set for a long run on television.

With income from all these sources, David had earned over $250,000 after expenses during 1971 – a sizeable sum for a young man of 21 trying to get ahead in the world.

Marriage? He didn't really want to think of that now.

When his dad and Shirley separated, he refused to take sides, for both his father and stepmother were very dear to him, and he hoped with all his heart that things could still be worked out – that Shirley and Jack would get back together.

But in the meantime, Jack was in New York, while Shirley's mother was staying with her in the Cassidys' beautiful home in Beverly Hills, where his three young half-brothers had now learned, as David had many years before them, the sadness of not having a father living at home.

As for David, at least he would still be working with Shirley six months out of every year on *The Partridge Family*, would still be playing her son, whatever his status as her stepson, and would still be friends with her.

He would be grateful to Shirley all his life for the warm and considerate way in which she had befriended a lonely seven-year-old boy whose father wasn't living with him anymore, and had taken him into her home for visits which showed him that his dad still loved him, and that his stepmother cared for him very much. He would never forget that. Not ever.

Why did he always lose the people he cared for? First his

father had gone away. Then his stepfather had moved out of the house after they had become good friends. And now he might lose Shirley as a stepmother.

Was this what marriage did to people? How could it break his heart three times?

And yet, if marriage seemed a remote possibility at the moment, romance did not.

At Cortina d'Ampezzo in the Italian Alps, David Cassidy took up skiing – accompanied by a delightful companion, a beautiful young girl from Florence.

Romance in the mountains of Italy ... a new experience, a wonderful memory to take back home when his all-too-brief vacation was over. Things were beginning to look better ... *much* better. And David Cassidy began to enjoy himself.

*Chapter Eighteen*

## DAVID'S HOPES AND
## FEARS FOR THE FUTURE

David Cassidy has always been one to plan for the future. Even when he was a lonely little boy with big, thick glasses and eyes that didn't look quite right, he was already planning for the day when he would be a star.

He sang in his church choir, seized at the chance to play bit parts in summer stock and soap operas, and practiced at home on the set of drums that his neighbor, Sal Mineo, had given him – the same drums that Sal had used in his starring performance in *The Gene Krupa Story*.

Maybe nobody else at that time believed that David would be a star, but David did. And not only did he believe it, he did something about it.

In high school, hopelessly behind in his studies, wracked by personal unhappiness, when things looked blackest, he never doubted for a moment that he would achieve stardom someday.

As you have seen in this book, that faith may have been the only thing that kept him from giving up and becoming a dropout from life, as he himself once put it. Others of his age found life too much to cope with and fell by the wayside, some of them in a very tragic fashion. But David had a goal that would not let him quit.

And today he continues to practice and improve constantly, to insure that his success will last as he goes on to other phases of his career.

Like Frank Sinatra and Elvis Presley before him, David Cassidy may well built himself an even brighter future in tomorrow's show business that goes far beyond his current fame as a teenage idol – a kind of fame he knows is fleeting in most cases.

Ironically, now that David has already achieved far more as an actor and singer than even *he* dared dream of in his early teens, he has moments when he is pessimistic – not only about his own future, but about the future of all mankind. For he is a member of a generation that really cares about others.

As I noted at the beginning of this book, when David was fifteen years old, I asked him what he wanted to be when he grew up, and he confidently told me that he wanted to be an actor. I was totally surprised by his answer.

When he was in his early twenties and already beginning to achieve his great success as a star on *The Partridge Family*, I asked him on the set one day, "What are some of the *other* things you want to do with your life?" And once again his answer surprised me – but for the opposite reason.

For this time he was more thoughtful than I'd ever seen him before, and seemingly a bit unsure of himself as he answered: "Oh, I've been writing music, and ... I don't know. Whatever happens! I'd like to travel and see a lot of things before they're not here anymore."

Perhaps that was why, as soon as his success had been assured and he had some money in his jeans, he took off for Europe to see the Continent in a camper during one of his vacations from *The Partridge Family*.

'Do you feel kind of pessimistic about the state of the world?' I asked him that day on the set of his show, as we discussed his future. For I sensed a pessimism in his words and in his manner.

"Yeah," he admitted quickly. "I think we're going to destroy ourselves, I really do ... if we keep going the way we're going, that is.

"I don't know if we'll really let ourselves, but I think it's
152

going to take people actually dying from air pollution before we really do something about it ... before they say, 'You can't run a car for a week,' or 'GM can no longer make this kind of car,' or 'Ford can no longer make this kind of car.'

"You know, they can *do* it if it's a matter of life and death and the end of the world," David emphasized. "I mean, people can do *anything* if they try!" Suddenly he was more hopeful, as he pointed out that the final pollution crisis *can* be avoided if people really do something about it in time.

"You know, I'm not a big crusader against air pollution," David admitted. "But I just don't like to *breathe* when I'm here in Los Angeles. And it's really depressing to wake up where I live and not be able to see the city at all!"

When I suggested that Santa Monica, the nearby seaside city in which I live, had not yet been polluted as badly as Los Angeles, David scoffed. "Are you kidding? It's the *worst* there. I've been there, and it's bad."

Perhaps he had seen the occasional brown vapors hanging over the sea in the sunset, a sunset strangely made more beautiful by the ominous colors of pollution.

"I just don't want to live in Los Angeles," David said firmly. "I've thought of moving to Canada or the Midwest or somewhere.

"But I believe in *action*, not in escape. I think that *anybody* who feels strongly about something should do it. You get a bunch of people together, and it keeps growing and growing — and eventually it's going to be heard!"

But he warned that organizing is all-important. "One person usually means nothing, really, you know? You can write your senator or congressman until you're blue in the face, and it really doesn't mean that much. People have to get together and work!"

At that moment David saw a woman signaling to him,

153

and we had to end our conversation, for he was needed elsewhere. But his next words, though casual, supplied a note of hope when I thought about them later.

"I have to go and do a tape for her to help the March of Dimes," David told me, and we said our goodbyes.

*"I have to do a tape to help the March of Dimes."* In the midst of his pessimistic appraisal of the future of the world, and his criticism of himself for not "getting involved" to help mankind, David had to break off the discussion – in order to go and *do* something to help that very world whose prospects he had called so bleak a few moments before.

For he had agreed to serve as a youth chairman for the March of Dimes. And somehow, between our discussion and his next call before the cameras to film a scene for *The Partridge Family*, he would find the time and energy to squeeze in some work for a charity that especially helps children and young people to be healthy and whole – and, through them, helps the world's future. He would be devoting many hours to that cause in the months to come despite his own crushing schedule.

That is so typical of the David Cassidy I know so well – and so typical of youth in general! While taking a sometimes pessimistic view of the future of the world as a whole, David works night and day to build his own future by entertaining that weary world, and then still finds time to help children and others younger than he, towards whom he has such a warm personal feeling.

It is as if he is saying, "I as one individual may not be able to fix what's wrong with the world. But at least I can do my best to help those who *may* someday save the world – the children and the very young."

And that was why our discussion had, after all, ended on a surprisingly revealing note of hope. For David Cassidy, despite the mess he thinks the world is in today, still believes deep down in his heart that there *will* be a tomorrow.

And, while modestly blaming himself for not doing enough to help our troubled world, in truth he is going

154

quietly about his way, working to make a better tomorrow come true.

But to do this he needs *your* help. Will you join David in making this a better world?

## HE GOT IT ALL TOGETHER

Looking back over these pages, it suddenly became clear to their author that the story of David Cassidy is in many ways the story of his generation, its problems and its achievements.

It is all there is that one life: the generation gap ... broken families ... fear of being "just a number ... drug temptations ... alienation and "dropping out" ... racial problems .. concern about pollution and overpopulation .. doubts about marriage ... uncertainty about the future in a world of war and crisis ... and yet, despite it all, the creation by the young of a brand-new way of life .. concern for the world's unfortunates ... radical changes in clothes and hair styles ... the development of rock 'n' roll as the music of a whole generation ... and a determination to go ahead with living, whatever the risks of life in our world today and tomorrow.

That is why, in a very real way, the story of David Cassidy is *your* story. For you and your friends, like David, are living through some of the most exciting and challenging times in the history of the world.

David Cassidy picked up that challenge and, with tremendous willpower and the use of his natural talents, he got it all together, carving out a place for himself where the whole world could see him.

It didn't happen because his father and stepmother were stars. His family helped with advice and encouragement, as any good family would, and their knowledge of show business was valuable in helping him steer clear of its various pitfalls. And his mother helped him with early training. But they couldn't get up there on stage and perform for him, and

David crashed Broadway on his own. There he was seen by a Hollywood talent scout, and his other breaks followed directly from that.

Nobody who knew David when he was in his early teens – with the exception of a loving mother – ever dreamed that he could reach the heights he has attained. But David Cassidy, who started out as an undersized, sickly, cross-eyed kid with thick glasses, believed it. And he made it all come true. He literally *transformed* himself through hard work and faith.

In doing so, he taught all of us who have been his friends since those early days a valuable lesson:

Never underestimate the ability of any human being to achieve miracles. Above all, never doubt your *own* ability to attain what you want in life, however fantastic your dreams may seem, as long as you are willing to work to make those dreams a reality.

David Cassidy did it. And if *he* did, take it from a startled friend of his . . . so can you!